ECONOMIC ISSUES, PROBLEMS AND PERSPECTIVES

PENSION BENEFIT GUARANTY CORPORATION

PREMIUM ISSUES

ECONOMIC ISSUES, PROBLEMS AND PERSPECTIVES

RETIREMENT ISSUES, PLANS AND LIFESTYLES

ECONOMIC ISSUES, PROBLEMS AND PERSPECTIVES

PENSION BENEFIT GUARANTY CORPORATION

PREMIUM ISSUES

STAN DUPONT
EDITOR

nova publishers
New York

Library of Congress Cataloging-in-Publication Data

ISBN: 978-1-62808-107-7

Published by Nova Science Publishers, Inc. † New York

CONTENTS

PREFACE

This book provides background and analysis of the premiums charged by the Pension Benefit Guaranty Corporation (PBGC), which is a government-owned corporation that was created in 1974 to protect the retirement income of participants in private-sector, defined benefit (DB) pension plans. When a company terminates a DB pension plan that does not have enough assets to pay 100% of the promised benefits, PBGC pays, in accordance with statute and up to a maximum yearly dollar amount, the benefits to participants in the terminated plan. In FY2012, 887,000 individuals received $5.5 billion in benefit payments from PBGC. An additional 614,000 workers will receive benefits when they retire. PBGC consists of two insurance programs: (1) a multiemployer pension program, which protects the benefits of 10.3 million participants in collectively bargained DB pensions in which several employers make contributions, and (2) a larger single-employer pension program, which protects the benefits of 33.4 million participants in DB pensions operated by one employer for its eligible employees.

Chapter 1 - This report provides background and analysis of the premiums charged by the Pension Benefit Guaranty Corporation (PBGC), which is a government-owned corporation that was created in 1974 to protect the retirement income of participants in private-sector, defined benefit (DB) pension plans. When a company terminates a DB pension plan that does not have enough assets to pay 100% of the promised benefits, PBGC pays, in accordance with statute and up to a maximum yearly dollar amount, the benefits to participants in the terminated plan. In FY2012, 887,000 individuals received $5.5 billion in benefit payments from PBGC. An additional 614,000 workers will receive benefits when they retire.

PBGC consists of two insurance programs: (1) a multiemployer pension program, which protects the benefits of 10.3 million participants in collectively bargained DB pensions in which several employers make contributions, and (2) a larger single-employer pension program, which protects the benefits of 33.4 million participants in DB pensions operated by one employer for its eligible employees. Since FY2002, PBGC has ended each fiscal year with a deficit. The total deficit for the PBGC at the end of FY2012 was $34.4 billion. Most of this deficit is attributable to the single-employer program, which ended FY2012 with a deficit of $29.1 billion. At the end of FY2012, PBGC's single-employer program reported assets of $83.0 billion and liabilities of $112.1 billion. Most of PBGC's liabilities are future benefit obligations.

Although PBGC receives no congressional appropriations, its financial condition may be of interest to Congress. If PBGC's deficit persists, then cuts to benefits or U.S. government financial assistance could be necessary. PBGC is funded by a combination of insurance premiums paid by employers who sponsor DB pension plans, the assets of DB pension plans that are trusteed by PBGC, and income earned on the investment of the trusteed plan assets.

Some policymakers who are concerned by PBGC's financial position have renewed the calls for changes to the structure of the premiums that PBGC collects from employers. The suggested changes include increasing current premium levels or adding a premium that would better reflect a pension plan's potential liability to PBGC. Currently, PBGC collects three premiums from DB plan sponsors: (1) an annual flat-rate premium of $42 per participant; (2) an annual variable-rate premium of $9 per $1,000 of underfunding; or (3) a termination premium of $1,250 per plan participant per year for three years for pension plans that terminate under certain conditions. Changes to PBGC's premium structure were included in the Department of Labor's FY2012 and FY2013 proposed budgets. In the 112th Congress, H.Con.Res. 34, the Concurrent Resolution of the Budget for Fiscal Year 2012, and H.Con.Res. 112, the Concurrent Resolution of the Budget for Fiscal Year 2013, recognized a need to reform PBGC but did not adopt the President's budget recommendations. In the 112th Congress, the Moving Ahead for Progress in the 21st Century Act (MAP-21; P.L. 112-141) increased the premiums levels but did not change the structure of the premiums that DB plan sponsors pay. Proponents of changes to PBGC's premium structure argue that the current premium structure does not adequately reflect the risk to PBGC of some underfunded pension plans. Some have proposed that PBGC charge premiums based on the financial health of a DB plan sponsor. They argue that the pension plans of financially healthy plan sponsors are less likely to be terminated and trusteed by PBGC and should not have to pay the same amount in premiums as less financially healthy companies. Although risk-based premiums would better allocate the risk of termination among DB plan sponsors, their implementation would raise additional concerns.

Chapter 2 - At the end of fiscal year 2011, PBGC insured the pension benefits of 44 million U.S. workers, retirees, and beneficiaries in about 27,000 private defined benefit plans. PBGC's 2011 net accumulated deficit of $26 billion, coupled with future risks posed by plan sponsors and their plans, threatens PBGC's solvency. To help contain PBGC's deficit, Congress recently passed legislation increasing PBGC premiums. Beyond simply increasing rates, the administration has proposed granting PBGC authority to redesign its premium structure to more fully reflect the risk of new claims. To better understand the issues involved, GAO was asked to examine (1) the options available to adjust premiums to improve PBGC's financial condition; (2) the potential implications of adjusting premiums; and (3) the potential implementation challenges in moving to a more risk-based premium structure.

To conduct this work, GAO reviewed relevant legislation, analyzed PBGC premium data, and interviewed officials implementing other risk-based premium structures in this country and the United Kingdom, as well as numerous experts and plan sponsors reflecting a broad spectrum of perspectives on the topic.

Chapter 3 - Recent economic conditions have generated attention with respect to the Pension Benefit Guaranty Corporation (PBGC) and defined benefit pension plans, including the process for terminating plans. The Employee Retirement Income Security Act (ERISA) regulates plan terminations. It provides for three types of single-employer plan terminations—standard, distress, and involuntary—and imposes different responsibilities on the PBGC for each type.

A standard termination occurs when a plan administrator decides to terminate a plan that has assets sufficient to meet its benefit liabilities. The PBGC's involvement in a standard termination is minimal, with its role basically limited to confirming all legal requirements have been met. In a standard termination, the plan sponsor has no further liability to the PBGC or plan participants. The sponsor may be able to recapture any assets remaining after participants have received their share, although the reversion may be subject to tax.

A distress termination occurs when a plan administrator seeks to terminate a plan that does not have sufficient assets to cover all the benefits owed to plan participants and beneficiaries. The PBGC is responsible for ensuring that all criteria for termination have been met, as well as for determining whether the plan's assets are sufficient to pay the guarantied benefits and/or meet all benefit liabilities. Meanwhile, the plan sponsor and members of its controlled group are jointly and severally liable to the PBGC for the amount that the benefit liabilities exceed plan assets, with interest, at termination.

An involuntary termination occurs when the PBGC decides a plan should be terminated. The agency must initiate termination proceedings once it determines a plan does not have assets available to pay benefits currently due. It may seek termination under certain circumstances, including the plan has not met the minimum funding requirements; the plan will not be able to pay benefits when due; or the long-run loss to the PBGC may be expected to increase unreasonably if the plan is not terminated. In an involuntary termination, the sponsor and controlled group are jointly and severally liable to the PBGC for the unfunded liabilities.

The PBGC is broadly authorized to make any investigation it deems necessary to enforce ERISA and may assess a penalty against anyone who fails to provide a required notice or other material information. In addition, plan participants, beneficiaries, fiduciaries, and sponsors who are adversely affected by an action of another that violates the termination provisions may file suit in U.S. district court to enjoin the action or obtain other equitable relief. Employee organizations representing affected participants and beneficiaries are also able to file a claim, and the PBGC has the right to intervene in any action.

Finally, if the PBGC determines that a plan should not be terminated, it may stop the termination proceedings and restore the plan. It even has the authority to restore a terminated plan.

In: Pension Benefit Guaranty Corporation ISBN: 978-1-62808-107-7
Editor: Stan Dupont

Chapter 1

PROPOSALS TO CHANGE PENSION BENEFIT GUARANTY CORPORATION'S (PBGC) PREMIUM STRUCTURE: ISSUES FOR CONGRESS*

John J. Topoleski

SUMMARY

This report provides background and analysis of the premiums charged by the Pension Benefit Guaranty Corporation (PBGC), which is a government-owned corporation that was created in 1974 to protect the retirement income of participants in private-sector, defined benefit (DB) pension plans. When a company terminates a DB pension plan that does not have enough assets to pay 100% of the promised benefits, PBGC pays, in accordance with statute and up to a maximum yearly dollar amount, the benefits to participants in the terminated plan. In FY2012, 887,000 individuals received $5.5 billion in benefit payments from PBGC. An additional 614,000 workers will receive benefits when they retire.

PBGC consists of two insurance programs: (1) a multiemployer pension program, which protects the benefits of 10.3 million participants

* This is an edited, reformatted and augmented version of a Congressional Research Service publication, CRS Report for Congress R42521, from www.crs.gov, prepared for Members and Committees of Congress, dated February 14, 2013.

in collectively bargained DB pensions in which several employers make contributions, and (2) a larger single-employer pension program, which protects the benefits of 33.4 million participants in DB pensions operated by one employer for its eligible employees. Since FY2002, PBGC has ended each fiscal year with a deficit. The total deficit for the PBGC at the end of FY2012 was $34.4 billion. Most of this deficit is attributable to the single-employer program, which ended FY2012 with a deficit of $29.1 billion. At the end of FY2012, PBGC's single-employer program reported assets of $83.0 billion and liabilities of $112.1 billion. Most of PBGC's liabilities are future benefit obligations.

Although PBGC receives no congressional appropriations, its financial condition may be of interest to Congress. If PBGC's deficit persists, then cuts to benefits or U.S. government financial assistance could be necessary. PBGC is funded by a combination of insurance premiums paid by employers who sponsor DB pension plans, the assets of DB pension plans that are trusteed by PBGC, and income earned on the investment of the trusteed plan assets.

Some policymakers who are concerned by PBGC's financial position have renewed the calls for changes to the structure of the premiums that PBGC collects from employers. The suggested changes include increasing current premium levels or adding a premium that would better reflect a pension plan's potential liability to PBGC. Currently, PBGC collects three premiums from DB plan sponsors: (1) an annual flat-rate premium of $42 per participant; (2) an annual variable-rate premium of $9 per $1,000 of underfunding; or (3) a termination premium of $1,250 per plan participant per year for three years for pension plans that terminate under certain conditions. Changes to PBGC's premium structure were included in the Department of Labor's FY2012 and FY2013 proposed budgets. In the 112th Congress, H.Con.Res. 34, the Concurrent Resolution of the Budget for Fiscal Year 2012, and H.Con.Res. 112, the Concurrent Resolution of the Budget for Fiscal Year 2013, recognized a need to reform PBGC but did not adopt the President's budget recommendations. In the 112th Congress, the Moving Ahead for Progress in the 21st Century Act (MAP-21; P.L. 112-141) increased the premiums levels but did not change the structure of the premiums that DB plan sponsors pay. Proponents of changes to PBGC's premium structure argue that the current premium structure does not adequately reflect the risk to PBGC of some underfunded pension plans. Some have proposed that PBGC charge premiums based on the financial health of a DB plan sponsor. They argue that the pension plans of financially healthy plan sponsors are less likely to be terminated and trusteed by PBGC and should not have to pay the same amount in premiums as less financially healthy companies. Although risk-based premiums would better allocate the risk of termination among DB plan sponsors, their implementation would raise additional concerns.

BACKGROUND ON PBGC

The Pension Benefit Guaranty Corporation (PBGC) is a federal government agency established in 1974 by the Employee Retirement Income Security Act (ERISA; P.L. 93-406). PBGC was created to protect the pension benefits of participants and beneficiaries in private-sector, defined benefit (DB) pension plans. These pension plans provide a specified monthly benefit at retirement, usually either a percentage of salary or a flat dollar amount multiplied by years of service. PBGC does not insure the pension plans of churches, religious organizations, state and local governments, or the federal government. In addition, defined contribution (DC) plans, such as §401(k) plans, are not insured by PBGC. PBGC is headed by a director who is appointed by the President and confirmed by the Senate. The Secretary of Labor chairs PBGC's Board of Directors, with the Secretaries of Treasury and Commerce serving as board members.

PBGC runs two distinct insurance programs: one program for single-employer pension plans and a second for multiemployer plans. Single-employer plans are operated by one employer for the benefit of eligible employees of that company. Multiemployer plans are collectively bargained plans to which more than one company makes contributions. PBGC maintains separate reserve funds for each program. The single-employer program is the larger of the two programs. In FY2012, the single-employer program insured 32.5 million participants in 24,200 pension plans and the multiemployer program covered 10.4 million participants in about 1,450 pension plans.[1] *As there are no current proposals to change the structure of the premiums of the multiemployer program, the remainder of this report discusses only the single-employer program.* Although federal law states that the U.S. government is not liable for any of the debts incurred by PBGC, [2] many policymakers feel that the government would provide PBGC the necessary resources if its funds became insufficient to pay benefits to retirees.[3]

The financial condition of PBGC may be of interest to Congress for several reasons: (1) Congress has demonstrated a clear interest in the retirement income security of American workers, for example, by providing a variety of tax incentives to encourage employer and employee contributions to retirement plans (Congress established PBGC as a pillar of retirement income security); (2) the insolvency of PBGC could require decreases in retirees' promised benefits or U.S. financial assistance; (3) increases in PBGC premiums are scored by the Congressional Budget Office (CBO) as increases in government revenue.

A pension plan may terminate either voluntarily in a standard or in a distress termination or in an involuntary PBGC-initiated termination.[4] A standard termination of a pension plan occurs when a pension plan has sufficient assets from which to pay participants' promised benefits. The pension plan sponsor guarantees benefits by purchasing an insurance annuity for each participant. PBGC's involvement in a standard termination is minimal: it confirms that the plan sponsor has met the requirements for conducting a standard termination. A distress termination of a pension plan occurs when a plan terminates with an insufficient amount of assets from which to pay participants' promised benefits. Employers cannot terminate an underfunded pension plan at their discretion: they must prove that they are financially unable to support the pension plan. PBGC may also initiate a termination of a pension plan. In a PBGC-initiated pension plan termination, PBGC must demonstrate one of the following: (1) the plan has not met the minimum funding requirements; (2) the plan cannot pay current benefits when due; (3) a lump sum payment has been made to a participant who is a substantial owner of the sponsoring company; or (4) the loss to PBGC is expected to increase unreasonably if the plan is not terminated.

In distress and involuntary terminations, PBGC becomes the trustee of the terminated plan and pays the participants' benefits in accordance to law and up to a statutory maximum benefit amount. PBGC guarantees the basic benefits of a pension plan, which include the pension benefits at normal retirement age, most early retirement benefits, disability benefits, and annuity benefits for survivors of plan participants. Some benefits are not fully guaranteed by PBGC.[5] PBGC cannot pay benefits to a retiree above a statutory maximum dollar amount. The maximum benefit depends upon the year of plan termination, the age at which the participant begins to receive benefits, and the form of the benefit payment. For example, the maximum benefit is $57,477 for a participant in a plan that is terminated in 2013 and who receives a single-life annuity beginning at the age of 65. The maximum benefit is $3,278 if the participant receives a joint-and-survivor annuity beginning at the age of 55 and the participant's spouse is also 55 years old.[6] PBGC reported in 2006 that an examination of 125 trusteed plans showed that 84% of participants received 100% of their benefits earned under the plan.[7]

The remainder of this report details the financial position and sources of revenue of the PBGC's single-employer pension program, describes the premiums that the sponsors of single-employer pension plans pay to PBGC, and discusses recent policy proposals to alter the structure of the premiums that single-employer pension plans pay to PBGC.

The Financial Position of PBGC

At the end of FY2012, the single-employer program of PBGC reported total assets of $83.0 billion of which $72.7 billion were investments. The remaining assets consisted of cash, securities lending collateral, receivables, and capitalized assets. PBGC reported total liabilities of $112.1 billion, of which $105.6 billion were the present value of future benefit payments. The total deficit of the single-employer program at the end of FY2012 was $29.1 billion.[8]

Table 1 details the amount of assets, liabilities, and the net financial position of PBGC's single-employer program from FY1980 to FY2012. From FY1980 to FY1994, PBGC had end of year deficits and from FY1995 to FY2001, PBGC finished each year with a surplus. Since FY2002, PBGC has reported yearly deficits at the end of the fiscal year. One measure of the financial health of a pension plan is the "funding ratio," which is the ratio of pension plan assets to liabilities. The ratio of assets to liabilities for PBGC was 74.0% at the end of FY2012, which means that currently PBGC has insufficient assets from which to fund all of its future benefit obligations.

Because the benefit obligations are paid out over several decades, retirees' benefits are not at immediate risk and PBGC has indicated that it "has enough funds to meet its obligations for years."[9] At the end of FY2012, PBGC had $83.0 billion in assets in its single-employer program and had paid $5.3 billion in benefits during FY2012. However, the deficit cannot persist indefinitely without an increase in PBGC revenues, a decrease in benefit outlays, or both.

The funding ratios of private-sector DB pension plans have been below 100% in recent years and continued weakness in the economy could result in increases in pension plan terminations. Greater pension plan underfunding implies that, on average, plans that end in distress terminations would impose a greater financial burden on PBGC. A study of the 100 largest corporate DB plans indicated that the funding ratios of these plans were 74.0% as of November 30, 2012.[10] The funded status of these plans was 105.4% in 2007, dropped to 79.3% in 2008, was 81.7% in 2009, 83.9% in 2010, and declined from 86.8% in February 2011 to 75.5% in February 2012. The decline in funding ratios since 2007 is the result of several factors: (1) new pension plan funding requirements authorized by the Pension Protection Act of 2006 (PPA; P.L. 109-280); (2) decrease in prices on the stock market, which reflected lower expectations for corporate profits due to the recession that began in December 2007 and ended in June 2009; and (3) lower interest rates, which reflected Federal Reserve efforts to influence the economic recovery.[11]

End of Fiscal Year: FY1980 to FY2012

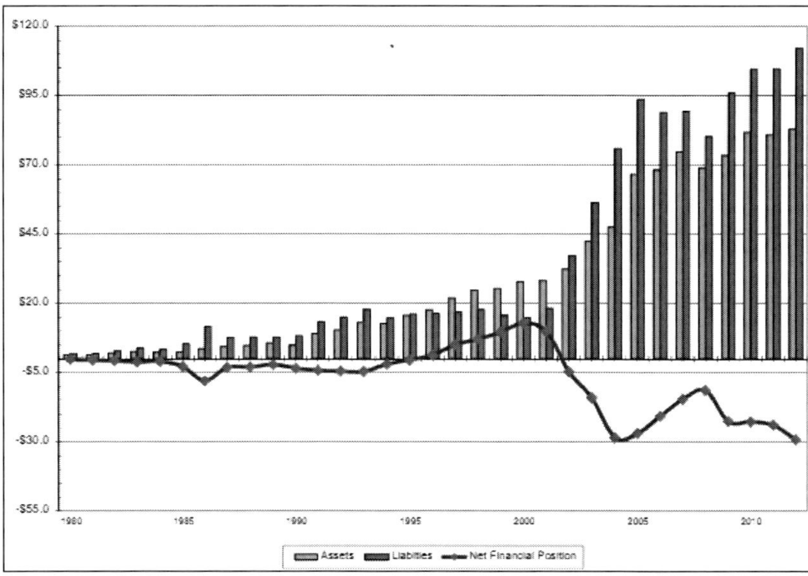

Source: PBGC Pension Insurance Data Books and FY2012 Annual Report.

Notes: CRS adjusted the dollar amounts for inflation using the fiscal year (October to September) monthly averages for the Consumer Price Index, All Urban Consumers (CPI-U).

Figure 1. Financial Position of the Single-Employer Insurance Program of the Pension Benefit Guaranty Corporation.

Table 1 provides information about the operations of PBGC's single-employer program since FY2003. Since its creation in 1974, PBGC has become the trustee of 4,447 single-employer pension plans and in FY2012 paid $5.4 billion in benefits to 781,160 end-of-FY2012 participants in these plans.[12] Over the past 10 years PBGC has become larger: it paid benefits to 1.4 times more participants in FY2012 than in FY2003 and paid 1.7 times more in inflation-adjusted benefit amounts in FY2012 than in FY2003.[13] PBGC's deficit increases with each pension plan that PBGC becomes trustee of, while the base from which PBGC collects premiums continues to decrease as a result of the increasing number of terminations of fully funded pension plans.[14]

Some policy analysts feel that certain PBGC accounting policies overstate its deficit.[15] For example, PBGC currently discounts its future benefits obligations using an interest rate that approximates the discount rate used in the private-sector annuity market. The rates used by PBGC were approximately 3.3% in FY2012.

Table 1. PBGC Single-Employer Program Data: FY2003 to FY2012

	FY2003	*FY2004*	*FY2005*	*FY2006*	*FY2007*	*FY2008*	*FY2009*	*FY2010*	*FY2011*	*FY2012*	*Percentage Change, 2003 - 2012*
Benefits Paid (millions of 2012 dollars)	$3,105.3	$3,666.7	$4,351.8	$4,649.5	$4,747.7	$4,573.4	$4,787.2	$5,747.6	$5,469.0	$5,384.0	*73.4%*
Participants Receiving Monthly Benefits[a]	458,800	517,900	682,540	612,630	631,130	640,070	743,610	747,530	775,300	781,160	*70.3%*
Number of Plans Trusteeship Trusteed and Pending	3,277	3,469	3,585	3,673	3,783	3,850	3,993	4,140	4,292	4,447	*35.7%*
Premium Income (millions of 2012 dollars)	$1,183.2	$1,778.4	$1,713.6	$1,642.5	$1,642.7	$1,427.9	$1,947.8	$2,345.5	$2,122.0	$2,642.0	*123.3%*
Investment Income (millions of 2012 dollars)	$4,179.9	$3,899.6	$4,602.2	$2,487.6	$5,271.9	-$4,437.0	$6,767.0	$7,983.8	$3,529.2	$8,792.0	-
Total Assets (millions of 2012 dollars)	$42,455.1	$47,562.9	$66,688.9	$68,309.5	$74,834.1	$68,848.9	$73,481.4	$81,438.9	$80,867.1	$82,973.0	*95.4%*
Present Value of Future Benefits (millions of 2012 dollars)	$55,716.1	$74,206.6	$82,356.7	$78,755.4	$77,053.3	$63,930.2	$88,767.6	$94,642.5	$95,198.0	$105,635.0	*89.6%*

Table 1. (Continued)

	FY2003	*FY2004*	*FY2005*	*FY2006*	*FY2007*	*FY2008*	*FY2009*	*FY2010*	*FY2011*	*FY2012*	*Percentage Change, 2003 - 2012*
Net Position: Assets –Liabilities[0] (millions of 2012 dollars)	-$14,026.1	-$28,427.0	-$26,897.6	-$20,664.1	-$14,591.5	-$11,378.2	-$22,532.1	-$22,702.3	-$23,827.9	-$29,142.0	-
Ratio of Assets to Liabilities	75.2%	62.6%	71.3%	76.8%	83.7%	85.8%	76.5%	78.2%	77.2%	74.0%	-

Source: FY2012 Annual Management Report.

Notes: CRS adjusted the dollar amounts for inflation using the FY (October to September) monthly averages for the Consumer Price Index, All Urban Consumers (CPI-U).

[a] This number refers to the number of participants receiving monthly benefits at the end of the fiscal year. Participants who received one-time, lump-sum payments or who died during the year are not counted.

[b] Besides the present value of future benefits, PBGC Annual Report includes the following payables as liabilities: derivative contracts, amounts due for purchases of securities, amounts payable upon return of securities loaned, unearned premiums, and accounts payable and accrued expenses. See the 2012 PBGC Annual Report available at http://www.pbgc.gov/documents/2012-annual-report.pdf.

Some have suggested that PBGC should value its benefit obligations using discount rates similar to the rates used by private-sector DB pension plans, which, in general, are higher than the insurance company rates that PBGC currently uses. Although the value of PBGC's benefit obligations would decrease if it used higher discount rates, PBGC's director indicated that he felt that current accounting practices should be maintained. He also indicated in February 2012 that discounting future benefit obligations using corporate bond rates would have lowered PBGC deficit to about $20 billion.16 Policy analysts have differences of opinion with regards to the appropriate rate for discounting pension plan liabilities.[17]

BANKRUPTCY OF AMERICAN AIRLINES AND EFFECT ON PBGC

The termination of several large and underfunded pension plans has contributed to PBGC's financial difficulties. Nine of the 10 largest claims since PBGC was established have occurred since 2001. Of the 10 companies, 5 were airlines, 4 were steel companies, and 1 was an automotive parts supplier. [18] Partly as a result of these large terminations, the present value of future benefits owed to PBGC participants doubled from 2002 to 2004.

American Airlines declared bankruptcy on November 28, 2011, and if its DB pension plans were terminated, these plans would represent the single largest claim on PBGC. In a press release dated November 29, 2011, PBGC indicated that "as of today, the plans collectively had about $8.3 billion in assets to cover about $18.5 billion in benefits. If American Airlines were to end their plans, the agency would be responsible for paying about $17 billion in benefits; about $1 billion in benefits would be lost."[19]

On March 7, 2012, American Airlines indicated that it would seek to freeze rather than terminate the three pension plans for employees who are not airline pilots.[20] American Airlines said that it would continue to seek a solution that would allow it to freeze rather than terminate the pilot pension plans.[21] In a press release dated March 7, 2012, PBGC said that "it is great progress and good news that American recognizes it can reorganize successfully and preserve its employees' pension plans. We're also glad the company is willing to work with us to preserve their pilot plan too."[22]

On December 14, 2012, PBGC submitted a statement to the United States Bankruptcy Court in support of an American Airlines' proposal to eliminate from the pilots' pension plan the option to receive benefits as a lump-sum benefit.[23] PBGC indicated that this action was necessary to avoid the termination of the pilots' pension plan.[24]

FINANCING OF PBGC

PBGC is entirely self-financing and does not receive any federal appropriations. PBGC is funded by cash flows from the premiums that pension plan sponsors pay, the assets of pension plans that are trusteed by PBGC, and dividends and interest from investments.

Revolving and Trust Funds

PBGC maintains three funds for the single-employer program: two on-budget revolving funds and a nonbudgetary trust fund.[25] The on-budget funds appear on the balance sheet of the federal government and changes to the revolving funds affect the federal budget deficit. The nonbudgetary trust fund does not appear on the balance sheet of the federal government and changes to the trust fund do not affect the federal budget deficit.

The revolving funds are on-budget accounts that receive the premiums that plan sponsors pay, earn interest income from investments in government securities, and receive transfers from the off-budget trust fund. Benefit payments are paid from the revolving funds. The assets of the revolving funds must be invested in U.S. government securities.

The nonbudgetary trust fund receives the assets of pension plans that are trusteed by PBGC. The assets in this trust fund are invested according to an investment policy approved by PBGC Board of Governors and are currently invested 30% in equities and 70% in fixed-income securities. The investment income earned by the trust fund is not counted as part of the federal budget. PBGC periodically transfers assets from the trust fund to the revolving fund to reimburse the payment of participant benefits.

PBGC premium income, interest on federal securities in PBGC's revolving funds, and transfers from PBGC's trust fund to PBGC's revolving fund are recorded as offsetting collections in the federal budget. Increases in these offsetting collections are recorded as increases in federal revenues.

PBGC Premiums

Each sponsor of a pension plan that is insured by PBGC pays annual premiums. Total premium income in FY2012 was approximately $2.6 billion, which was 49.1% of the amount of benefits paid.[26] For FY2003 to FY2012, premium income averaged 39.7% of benefits paid.

Three Types of PBGC Premiums

PBGC collects three types of premiums: (1) a flat-rate, per participant premium, (2) a variable-rate premium based on the dollar amount of a plan's underfunding, and (3) a per-participant premium payable for three years after a DB pension plan terminates. The premium amounts are authorized in 29 U.S.C. 1306. Changes in PBGC's premium structure and changes to premium amounts have been authorized by Congress in statute, although previous Administrations have proposed giving PBGC's Board of Directors the authority to set premium levels.[27]

- *Flat-rate premium.* The sponsors of DB pension plans pay annual premiums of $42 per participant. The premium amount is indexed to increases in the national average wage index, as determined by the Social Security Administration. The flat rate premium was last increased in 2009. In FY2012, PBGC collected $1.1 billion in flat-rate premiums. This premium was authorized by ERISA and was initially set at $1.00 per participant.
- *Variable-rate premium.* Plans that do not have enough assets set aside to pay 100% of the promised benefits are considered underfunded. The sponsors of underfunded DB plans pay an annual premium of $9 per $1,000 of underfunding.[28] Beginning in 2014, the variable-rate premium will be indexed to increases in the average wage index. In FY2012, PBGC collected $1.5 billion in variable rate premiums. In FY2010, the most recent year for which PBGC has published data, 41.7% of insured pension plans paid the variable-rate premium and 48.9% of participants in insured plans were in plans paying the variable-rate premium.[29] This premium was authorized in the Omnibus Budget Reconciliation Act of 1987 (P.L. 100-203).
- *Termination premium.* Plans that terminate under certain distress terminations or in a PBGC initiated termination are liable for a termination premium of $1,250 per plan participant per year for three years. This premium was authorized in the Deficit Reduction Act of

2005 (P.L. 109-171) and was scheduled to expire December 31, 2010; however, the Pension Protection Act of 2006 (PPA; P.L. 109-280) made this premium permanent. In FY2012, PBGC recorded $237 million in termination premiums, which were offset by $207 million in write-offs of interest, penalties, and termination premiums. PBGC indicated that it does not expect to collect termination premiums and indicated that "the termination premium is reserved at 100% since no significant collection has yet been achieved."[30]

In addition to premium income, in FY2012, PBGC also collected $5 million in interest and penalties and wrote-off $207 million in interest, penalties, and termination premiums that it does not expect to collect. Net premium income in FY2012 was $2.6 billion.

ERISA established the initial flat-rate premium of $1.00 per participant and the $2.60 flat-rate premium beginning in 1978. The variable rate premium was first collected in 1988 and the termination premium was first collected in 2006. Since 2007, the flat-rate premium has been adjusted annually for increases in the national average wage index, as determined by the Social Security Administration. Beginning in 2014 the variable-rate premium will also be adjusted for increases in the national wage index. The changes to the index were insufficient for an increase in the flat-rate premium in 2011 or 2012.

Some policymakers have suggested that PBGC premiums are lower than those that would be charged in a private market. For example, a research paper in 2002 estimated that private insurance premiums would be twice the amount charged by the PBGC at the time.[31]

A 2005 report by CBO indicated that premiums would need to be increased by a factor of 6.5 to be comparable to premiums charged in a private insurance market.[32]

Table 2 provides historical data on the single-employer program premium levels.

Table 2. PBGC Single-Employer Program Premium Levels

		Authorizing Statute	*Flat-Rate Premium*	*Variable-rate Premium*	*Termination Premium*
September 2, 1974	– 1977	Employee Retirement Income	$1.00	-	-
		Security Act of 1974			

		Authorizing Statute	*Flat-Rate Premium*	*Variable-rate Premium*	*Termination Premium*
		(ERISA; P.L. 93-406)			
1978 – 1985			$2.60[a]	-	-
1986 – 1987		Consolidated Omnibus Budget	$8.50	-	-
		Reconciliation Act of 1985(P.L. 99-272)			
1988 – 1990		Omnibus Budget	$16.00	$6.00	-
		Reconciliation Act of 1987(P.L. 100-203)			
1991 – 2005		Omnibus Budget	$19,00	$9.00	-
		Reconciliation Act of 1990(P.L. 101-508)			
2006		Deficit Reduction Act of 2005(P.L. 109-171)	$30.00	$9.00	$1,250.00
2007			$31.00[b]	$9.00	$1,250.00[c]
2008			$33.00	$9.00	$1,250.00
2009			$34.00	$9.00	$1,250.00
2010 - 2012			$35.00	$9.00	$1,250.00
2013			$42.00	$9.00	$1,250.00
2014			$49.00	[e]	$1,250.00
2015			[d]	[e]	$1,250.00

Source: Congressional Research Service.

[a] The Employee Retirement Income Security Act of 1974 (ERISA; P.L. 93-406) established the initial premium rate of $1.00 per participant. ERISA authorized the increase in the flat-rate premium to $2.60 beginning in 1978.

[b] The Deficit Reduction Act of 2005 (P.L. 109-171) adjusted the flat-rate premium annually for increases in the national wage index beginning in 2007.

[c] The Pension Protection Act of 2006 (PPA; P.L. 109-280) provided for a special termination premium of $2,500 per participant for pension plans of commercial airlines that terminated within a five-year period that began with the year that a commercial airline plan adopted funding rules made available to commercial airlines in the PPA.

[d] The flat-rate premium in 2015 will be adjusted for changes in the national wage index in 2014.

[e] MAP-21 increased the variable-rate premium by $4 (after the 2013 level is adjusted for changes in the national wage index) per $1,000 of unfunded benefits in 2014, and by another $5 (after the 2014 level is adjusted for changes in the national wage index) per $1,000 of unfunded vested benefits in 2015.

Proposals to Adjust PBGC's Premium Structure

Since 2002, PBGC has reported end of fiscal year deficits. Recently, some policymakers have suggested changes to PBGC premiums to eliminate the deficit and minimize the likelihood that PBGC would exhaust its resources. If the PBGC were unable to make benefits payments, it might need to implement changes to participants' benefits or request financial assistance.

In the 112th Congress, The Moving Ahead for Progress in the 21st Century Act (MAP-21; P.L. 112-141) increased flat-rate and variable-rate premiums that DB plan sponsors pay. MAP-21 did not alter the structure of the premiums.

The following are some recent policy proposals that would affect PBGC premiums:

- *President Barack Obama's FY2012 and FY2013 Budgets.* TheAdministration's FY2012 and FY2013 budgets for the Department of Labor proposed that PBGC Board receive authority to adjust premiums and to take into account the risks that different sponsors pose to PBGC. Specifically, the FY2013 Budget proposed giving PBGC Board the authority to set premiums beginning in 2014. The budget also called for a one-year study and public comment period to assist with implementation and a gradual phase-in of premium increases. The Administration estimates that this proposal would save $16 billion over 10 years.[33] PBGC's director indicated that premiums average about 3.5 cents per hour for an industrial worker and that increases in the premiums would be a small percentage of hourly wages.[34]
- *House FY2012 and FY2013 Budget Proposals.* The reports to H.Con.Res. 34, the Concurrent Resolution of the Budget for Fiscal Year 2012, which was passed by the House on April 15, 2011, and H.Con.Res. 112, the Concurrent Resolution of the Budget for Fiscal Year 2013, which was passed by the House on March 29, 2012, contained identical language that stated they did not assume the President's proposal but "recognized the need to reform PBGC to ensure that a future taxpayer funded bailout does not occur." The budget resolutions estimated potential savings over 10 years of $2.7 billion (in the FY2012 budget resolution) and $8.34 billion (in the FY2013 budget resolution) but did not indentify the source of the savings.[35]

- *The President's Plan for Economic Growth and Deficit Reduction.* In September 2011, the President's proposal to the Joint Select Committee on Deficit Reduction was released and contained legislative language that would have increased the flat-rate premium from the current rate of $35 per participant per year to $44 per participant in 2014. The flat-rate premium would have increased each year until 2020 to $66 per participant per year. The proposal would have replaced the variable-rate premium that is based on the amount of plan underfunding with a risk-based premium that would have been determined by the following factors: the risk of losses to PBGC; a plan's assets and liabilities; the financial condition of the plan's sponsor; PBGC estimated investment income; and any other factor PBGC's Board would have determined to be appropriate. The proposal also recommended that increases in the premiums would have been minimized when the economy or financial markets were weak. In addition, the proposal would have prohibited reliance on credit agency ratings to set premiums, although publically available measures of risk or exposure could have been used. The proposal also would have prohibited premium increases that resulted in premiums more than four times as large as a plan sponsor's 2010 premium.[36]
- *The National Commission on Fiscal Responsibly and Reform.* The report from the National Commission on Fiscal Responsibly and Reform, co-chaired by former Senator Alan Simpson and Erskine Bowles and released in December 2010, contained a recommendation that PBGC's board be given authority to increase the flat-rate and variable-rate premiums.[37]
- *The Debt Reduction Task Force.* The Debt Reduction Task Force, co-chaired by former Senator Pete Domenici and Alice Rivlin and released in November 2010, recommended that the flat-rate premium increase by 15% (which would increase the premium from $35 to $40.25) and that the variable-rate premium increase from $9 to $12 per $1,000 of underfunding.[38] The task force also recommended that the variable rate premium be based partly on the riskiness of a pension plan's investment allocation. Pension plans that have a greater allocation in equities would pay higher variable rate premiums.[39]

Analysis of PBGC Premiums and Proposed Changes

The $23.3 billion FY2012 deficit in PBGC's single-employer program has renewed focus on the financing of PBGC and the premiums that Congress has authorized PBGC to collect. Changes to PBGC's premium structure were also discussed as part of pension plan funding reforms prompted by the termination of several large pension plans in the early 2000s. Of the top 10 largest companies that have presented claims to PBGC, the termination of the pension plans of nine of these occurred from 2001 to 2005.

Although the current structure of flat-rate and variable-rate premiums has both advantages and disadvantages, premium changes would not be without potential challenges. This section discusses these issues and challenges, including the counter-cyclical nature of pension plan insurance, the challenges for PBGC in determining private-sector companies' financial health, and comparisons with other government insurance programs.

In response to higher pension insurance premiums, some pension plan sponsors might choose to freeze or terminate their DB pension plans. In a pension plan freeze, the pension plan is closed to new participants. In addition, a pension plan may opt to prohibit existing participants from earning pension benefits in the future. In a terminated pension plan, the plan sponsor closes the pension plan, but must guarantee participants' benefits through the purchase of an insurance annuity for each of the participants.

Flat-Rate Premiums

The flat-rate premium under current law has the advantage of being simple to calculate. This advantage was recognized by the Ford administration in 1974, which said that this type of premium would be

> the easiest approach to administer for both plan administrators and the insurance Corporation.... These aspects—simple calculation, prompt collection, and a fairly accurate estimate of how much money will be raised—will be very important for a sound and effective inauguration of the insurance program....
>
> While the head tax does very little to reflect insurance risk with regard to any given plan, it does not create serious inequities because it is virtually a nominal rate and will be in effect for only a few years. Any inequities in the early years will be smoothed out over the long run when the program operates under a more risk-based premium structure.[40]

The flat-rate premium is a disadvantage to plans that offer smaller per participant benefits. Plan sponsors pay this premium regardless of the size of benefits an individual would receive. This structure favors plans that offer greater per-participant benefits, who pay a lower premium per dollar of benefits covered. For example, one of the factors in a typical DB pension formula is the number of years of service a participant has with an employer. Pension plans with participants that have longer job tenure would tend to have larger benefit obligations than pension plans with workers with shorter job tenure.

Variable-Rate Premiums and Proposed Risk-Based Premiums

The variable rate premium, which is calculated on the dollar amount of pension plan underfunding, takes into account the fact that plans terminated with larger amounts of underfunding would increase PBGC's deficit more than plans with smaller amounts of underfunding. However, two pension plans with equal amounts of underfunding could pose different risks to PBGC depending on the financial health of the plan sponsor. For example, two pension plans could have an equal number of participants, pay equal benefits, and have an equal amount of underfunding but could pose different risks to the PBGC based on the financial condition of the plan sponsors: plan sponsors in weak financial condition are more likely to be terminated and trusteed by PBGC compared with the pension plans of plan sponsors in good financial condition.

PBGC Determinations of Financial Health of Companies in Risk-based Premium Structure

Premiums based on the financial health of a plan sponsor would require PBGC to make determinations regarding the risk of individual companies. It might be difficult to measure the financial health of some smaller firms. Large companies likely have public debt or publicly available financial statements. However smaller firms are less likely to have publicly available information or could find compiling required information administratively burdensome. Of the 27,647 single-employer pension plans insured by PBGC in FY2010, 16,695 (63.9%) had fewer than 100 participants.[41]

Countercyclical Nature of Variable-Rate and Risk-Based Premiums

A drawback of the variable-rate premium, and a potential drawback of risk-based premiums, is the amount of premiums that companies pay increases during economic downturns. The amount of variable-rate premiums would increase as a result of possible increases in pension plan underfunding, caused by declines in asset values and interest rates. If risk-based premiums are based on the financial health of a company, then these might also increase during economic downturns as firms are more likely to face financial difficulties during recessions. However, companies are more likely to need cash during economic downturns. Some could find paying higher pension insurance premiums during economic downtowns burdensome. The President's Plan for Economic Growth and Deficit Reduction recommended that premium increases be minimized during economic downturns.

Comparison with Other Government Insurance Programs

PBGC is one of several government-run insurance programs, including federal crop insurance, federal flood insurance, and insurance for banking deposits. The Federal Deposit Insurance Corporation (FDIC) and the National Credit Union Administration (NCUA) insure deposits in covered banks and credit unions. Some of these federal insurance programs have risk-based premiums.[42] For example, FDIC charges premiums based on the riskiness of a bank's assets. Generally, the riskier a bank's assets are then the more likely the bank is to fail, which suggests a greater likelihood that FDIC would be required to cover deposits of that bank.

However, FDIC's insurance model may not be fully applicable to pension insurance. The riskiness of a bank's financial condition may be easier to determine than the riskiness of nonfinancial companies. For example, the riskiness of a bank is determined by an examination of the kinds of financial assets that the bank owns, which tend to have standard measures of risk. It may be difficult to determine the riskiness of non-financial companies or to establish uniform standard for all companies across many different industries. For example, the ratio of a firm's debts to assets is a common financial indicator to measure a company's financial health: a firm with a large amount of debt may be more likely to default on its debt. However, the typical debt-to-assets ratio tends vary across industries. Firms in capital intensive industries (such as airlines) tend to have higher debt-to-assets ratios than firms in less capital intensive industries. Although many indicators of a company's financial health are potentially available, some amount of judgment by PBGC might be needed to make final determinations.

End Notes

[1] See the 2012 PBGC Annual Report available at http://www.pbgc.gov/documents/2012-annual-report.pdf.

[2] 29 U.S.C. 1302(g)(2) states that "The United States is not liable for any obligation or liability incurred by the corporation."

[3] See, for example, "$34 Billion Shortfall Estimate Sparks Renewed Talk of Taxpayer Help for PBGC," Pensions & Investments, May 14, 2010, available at http://www.pionline.com/article/20100514/REG/100519901.

[4] More information on pension plan terminations is available in CRS Report RS22624, The Pension Benefit Guaranty Corporation and Single-Employer Plan Terminations, by Jennifer Staman and Erika K. Lunder.

[5] For example, the PBGC does not guarantee benefits that were created or increased within five years prior to plan termination.

[6] The benefit is adjusted to be actuarially neutral. A benefit payment is actuarially neutral if it is adjusted to pay the same total dollar amount over a participant's expected lifetime.

[7] See Pension Insurance Data Book 2006, available at http://www.pbgc.gov/docs/2006 databook. pdf.

[8] See the 2012 PBGC Annual Report available at http://www.pbgc.gov/documents/2012-annual-report.pdf.

[9] See Message from Director Josh Gotbaum in PBGC 2012 Annual Report, available at http://www.pbgc.gov/ Documents/2012_annual_report.pdf.

[10] These studies cover the 100 U.S. public companies with the largest defined benefit pension assets. For data through the end of 2009 see Milliman 2010 Pension Funding Study available at http://www.milliman.com/expertise/employeebenefits/products-tools/pension-funding-study/pdfs/pension-funding-study.pdf. For data from 2010 and 2011 see the Milliman 100 Pension Funding Index available at http://publications.milliman.com/ publications/eb-published/pdfs/ milliman-100-pension-funding-01-06-12.pdf. For 2012 data see the Milliman 100 Pension Funding Index, available at http://milliman.com/expertise/ employee-benefits/products-tools/pension-funding-index/pdfs/pfi-january-2013.pdf.

[11] The S&P 500 stock market index declined 38% in 2008 and as of December 31, 2011, was 19% below its October 12, 2007, peak. One-year Treasury note yields were 5.0% on January 2, 2007, and had fallen to 0.12% on January 3, 2012.

[12] PBGC reported 755,300 benefits' recipients as of the end of FY2011. Approximately 873,000 retirees received a PBGC benefit in FY2011, some of whom received a one-time, lump-sum benefit or died before the end of the fiscal year.

[13] The nominal (not adjusted for inflation) amount was 3.5 times more in total benefits payments in FY2011 compared with FY2002.

[14] Although the number of participants who receive benefits and the number of plans trusteed by PBGC has increased since 2002, the number of participants in PBGC insured plans decreased from 34.2 million in FY2002 to 33.4 million in FY2011 and the number of plans covered decreased from 31,229 to 25,607 over the same period. See Tables S-30 and S-31 of the Pension Insurance Data Book 2009 for the number of PBGC-insured plans and the number of plan participants from 1980 to 2009. See the 2011 PBGC Annual Report for the number of PBGC-insured plans and the number of plan participants in 2010 and 2011, available at http://www.pbgc.gov/documents/2011-annual-report.pdf.

[15] See American Benefits Council, "Ten Reasons to Doubt PBGC's Reported Deficit," press release, November 15, 2011, available at http://www.appwp.org/newsroom/2011/pr11-18.cfm.

[16] Testimony of PBGC Director Joshua Gotbaum, in U.S. Congress, House Education and the Workforce Subcommittee on Health, Employment, Labor, and Pensions, Examining the Challenges Facing PBGC and Defined Benefit Pension Plans, Hearings, 112th Cong., 2nd sess., February 2, 2012.

[17] In general, financial economists tend to say that pension plans should use discounts rates that reflect the probability that a payment will not be made in the future while actuaries tend to say that pension plans should use discount rates that equal the expected rate of return on plan assets. PBGC's use of discount rates that insurance companies use are lower than the

discount rates used by private pension plans and much lower than those used by state and local government pension plans.

[18] The 10 companies, in order by size of claim, are United Airlines, Delphi, Bethlehem Steel, US Airways, LTV Steel, Delta Airlines, National Steel, Pan American Air, Trans World Airlines, and Weirton Steel.

[19] See "Statement from PBGC Director Josh Gotbaum on AMR Corp. Bankruptcy," available at http://www.pbgc.gov/ news/press/releases/pr12-08.html.

[20] A Q&A for American Airlines employees is available at http://www.aa.com/content/images/ amrcorp/ jjb_pension_letter_all.pdf.

[21] A Q&A for American Airlines pilots is available at http://www.aa.com/content/images/ amrcorp/ jjb_pension_letter_pilots.pdf.

[22] See "Statement From PBGC Director Josh Gotbaum on AMR Corp.'s Letter on Plan Freezes," available at http://www.pbgc.gov/news/press/releases/pr12-18.html.

[23] See Amendment of American Airlines Plan Needed To Avoid Termination, PBGC Tells Court, Pension and Benefits Daily, December 18, 2012, available at http://news.bna.com/pdln/ PDLNWB/split_display.adp?fedfid=28911873& vname=pbdnotallissues&wsn=495229500&searchid=19247636&doctypeid=1&type=date& mode=doc&split=0&scm= PDLNWB&pg=0.

[24] On November 7, 2012, the IRS issued a regulation which indicated that, under certain circumstances, a pension plan sponsor in bankruptcy may eliminate optional forms of benefits, such as lump-sum benefits, available in a pension plan if the plan sponsor. In general, under anti-cutback rules, pension plan sponsors may not eliminate benefits available under a pension plan. For more information, see IRS Issues Rule With Anti-Cutback Exception; Regulation May Save Airline's Pension Plan, Pension and Benefits Daily, November 8, 2012, available at http://news.bna.com/pdln/ PDLNWB/split_ display.adp?fedfid=28577206&vname=pbdnotallissues&wsn=495692500&searchid=19247 636& doctypeid=1&type=date&mode=doc&split=0&scm=PDLNWB&pg=0.

[25] ERISA Section 4005 (29 U.S.C. 1305) established seven revolving funds to carry out PBGC's activities. One of these funds supports activities in the multiemployer program and three of these funds are not used because PBGC currently does not carry out activities supported by these trust funds. Further information on the trust funds is available in U.S. General Accounting Office, Pension Benefit Guaranty Corporation: Statutory Limitation on Administrative Expenses Does Not Provide Meaningful Control, GAO-03-301, February 2003, http://www.gao.gov/new.items/ d03301.pdf.

[26] Benefit payments are made from premium income, investment income from the revolving and trust funds, and transfers from the trust fund.

[27] For example, the FY2008 Department of Labor budget indicated that the administration would introduce legislation to authorize PBGC's Board of Directors to set the variable premium rate. See Department of Labor FY2008 Budget, available at http://www.gpo.gov/fdsys/pkg/ BUDGET-2008-APP/pdf/BUDGET-2008-APP-1-15.pdf. Legislation was not introduced in the 110th Congress.

[28] Prior to 2008, underfunded DB plans that made a contribution to their pension plan equal to their full funding limit were not required to pay the variable premium. The full funding limit was the maximum tax deduction allowed by a plan for pension plan contributions.

[29] See 2010 pension insurance data tables available from PBGC at http://www.pbgc.gov/ Documents/pension-insurancedata-tables-2010.pdf.

[30] The PBGC income statement records a bad debt expense equal to 100% of the termination premium, plus an amount for uncollectable interest and penalties, because it does not expect

to collect termination premiums from plan sponsors. See PBGC FY2011 Annual Report, p. 75.

[31] See Steven Boyce and Richard A. Ippolito, "The Cost of Pension Insurance," Journal of Risk and Insurance, vol. 69, no. 2 (June 2002).

[32] See Congressional Budget Office, The Risk Exposure of the Pension Benefit Guaranty Corporation, September 2005.

[33] There have been previous calls for a change to risk-based premiums. For example, a 2005 proposal from the George W. Bush Administration to reform the defined benefit pension system included PBGC premiums based on the level of risk for financially troubled companies. See "Pension Reform: 'More Honey Than Vinegar' in President's Proposal, Official Says," Pension and Benefits Daily, The Bureau of National Affairs, January 18, 2005.

[34] Testimony of PBGC Director Joshua Gotbaum, in U.S. Congress, House Education and the Workforce Subcommittee on Health, Employment, Labor, and Pensions, Examining the Challenges Facing PBGC and Defined Benefit Pension Plans, hearings, 112th Cong., 2nd sess., February 2, 2012. In FY2011, PBGC reported revenues of $2.0 billion and that the single-employer program covered about 33.0 million defined benefit pension plan participants. The premium per worker in FY2011 was, on average, approximately $60 per year, although considerable variation likely exists in the per-person premiums. Plans that were 100% funded paid the $35 flat-rate premium, while underfunded plans paid the $35 flat-rate premium plus the variable-rate premium.

[35] See U.S. Congress, House Committee on the Budget, Concurrent Resolution on the Budget—Fiscal Year 2012, report to accompany H.Con.Res. 34, 112th Cong., 1st sess., H.Rept. 112-58 (Washington, DC: GPO, 2011), p. 108 and U.S. Congress, House Committee on the Budget, Concurrent Resolution on the Budget—Fiscal Year 2013, report to accompany H.Con.Res. 112, 112th Cong., 2nd sess., H.Rept. 112-421 (Washington, DC: GPO, 2011), p. 101.

[36] The recommendation is available at http://www.whitehouse.gov/sites/default/files/omb/budget/ fy2012/assets/ jointcommitteereport.pdf.

[37] See The Moment of Truth, available at http://www.fiscalcommission.gov/sites/ fiscal commission.gov/files/ documents/TheMomentofTruth12_1_2010.pdf.

[38] The report is available at http://www.bipartisanpolicy.org/sites/default/files/ BPC%20FINAL% 20REPORT%20FOR%20PRINTER%2002%2028%2011.pdf.

[39] Pension plans that have greater allocations in equities would be more likely to experience variation in their funding ratios because the value of equities (like stocks) tends to be more variable than the price of debt instruments (like bonds).

[40] Administration Recommendations to the House and Senate Conferees on H.R. 2 to Provide for Pension Reform, April 1974, available in U.S. Congress, Senate Committee on Labor, Subcommittee on Labor, and Public Welfare, Legislative History of the Employee Retirement Income Security Act of 1974: vol. III, committee print, 94th Cong., 2nd sess., April 1976, p. 5116 - 5117.

[41] See Pension Benefit Guaranty Corporation, Pension Insurance Data Tables 2010, Table S-31. As of April 25, 2012, PBGC had not released the Pension Insurance Data Books for 2011.

[42] More information on these programs is available in the following CRS reports: CRS Report R40532, Federal Crop Insurance: Background , by Dennis A. Shields; CRS Report R40650, National Flood Insurance Program: Background, Challenges, and Financial Status, by Rawle O. King; and CRS Report R41718, Federal Deposit Insurance for Banks and Credit Unions, by Darryl E. Getter and Victor Tineo.

In: Pension Benefit Guaranty Corporation
Editor: Stan Dupont
ISBN: 978-1-62808-107-7

Chapter 2

PENSION BENEFIT GUARANTY CORPORATION: REDESIGNED PREMIUM STRUCTURE COULD BETTER ALIGN RATES WITH RISK FROM PLAN SPONSORS*

United States Government Accountability Office

WHY GAO DID THIS STUDY

At the end of fiscal year 2011, PBGC insured the pension benefits of 44 million U.S. workers, retirees, and beneficiaries in about 27,000 private defined benefit plans. PBGC's 2011 net accumulated deficit of $26 billion, coupled with future risks posed by plan sponsors and their plans, threatens PBGC's solvency. To help contain PBGC's deficit, Congress recently passed legislation increasing PBGC premiums. Beyond simply increasing rates, the administration has proposed granting PBGC authority to redesign its premium structure to more fully reflect the risk of new claims. To better understand the issues involved, GAO was asked to examine (1) the options available to adjust premiums to improve PBGC's financial condition; (2) the potential implications of adjusting premiums; and (3) the potential implementation challenges in moving to a more risk-based premium structure.

---

* This is an edited, reformatted and augmented version of United States Government Accountability Office, Publication No. GAO-13-58, dated November 2012.

To conduct this work, GAO reviewed relevant legislation, analyzed PBGC premium data, and interviewed officials implementing other risk-based premium structures in this country and the United Kingdom, as well as numerous experts and plan sponsors reflecting a broad spectrum of perspectives on the topic.

WHAT GAO RECOMMENDS

GAO suggests that Congress consider revising PBGC's premium structure to better reflect the agency's risk from individual plans and sponsors, and recommends that PBGC further develop its analyses of possible redesign options. PBGC agreed with our recommendation.

WHAT GAO FOUND

Various options are available to make the Pension Benefit Guaranty Corporation's (PBGC) premium structure more risk-based and better reflect the risk of future claims. Historically, PBGC's premiums have not fully reflected the risks PBGC insures against—chiefly that a plan sponsor with an underfunded plan will become bankrupt, forcing the termination of the plan and imposing a claim on PBGC. PBGC's current structure relies largely on a flat-rate premium that is based on the number of plan participants and that assesses rates equally per plan participant across all sponsors. PBGC also charges a variable-rate premium that is based on just one risk factor, plan underfunding. One available option is to further increase rates within this current structure; however, plan underfunding alone is a poor proxy for the risk of new claims. An alternative option is to redesign premiums to incorporate additional risk factors, such as a sponsor's financial strength (as currently being explored by PBGC) or a plan's investment strategy (as is currently done in the United Kingdom).

Moving to a more risk-based system would shift premium costs among sponsors. To analyze the potential effects of different premium structures, PBGC developed a model using data from a sample of about 2,700 plans. Under one possible option explored by PBGC that incorporated an additional risk factor for a sponsor's financial health, financially healthier sponsors would tend to pay less and financially riskier sponsors more—as much as $257 more per participant, depending on their assigned risk level. Some pension experts and plan sponsors we spoke with raised concerns about this potential redistribution of costs. For example, some believe that plan terminations would increase. However, prior work from GAO and others indicates that other factors—including sponsor size, collective bargaining agreements, and overall plan cost—are more important in sponsors' decisions to freeze their plans. Some pension experts and plan sponsors also noted that a more risk-based system could lead to premium increases during poor economic conditions when sponsors are least able to pay, and that it is inequitable for current sponsors to pay higher rates to address costs resulting from prior plan terminations. However, experts also made suggestions about how to address such concerns within a redesigned premium structure, such as by capping premium levels and averaging sponsors' funding levels over multiple years to reduce volatility.

The process of redesigning and implementing a more risk-based premium structure poses potential data and administrative challenges. To help address these challenges, PBGC's model could be further developed to evaluate the implications of incorporating additional risk factors, such as company financial health and plan investment mix. Such efforts could include identifying any additional data needs, as well as exploring the effects on sponsors, including any potentially disproportional hardships on smaller companies resulting from redistributing higher rates to riskier sponsors based on a redesigned structure. Although PBGC is uniquely situated to take on additional rate-setting responsibilities, if Congress were to relinquish some authority in this area, certain safeguards still may be required to help mitigate concerns about PBGC's governance, oversight, and transparency. These safeguards could include additional congressional oversight, soliciting public feedback, and establishing an appeals process for sponsors who wish to challenge their assessment.

ABBREVIATIONS

CAMELS	capital, asset quality, management, earnings, liquidity, and sensitivity to market risk
CBO	Congressional Budget Office
DB	defined benefit
ERISA	Employee Retirement Income Security Act of 1974
FDIC	Federal Deposit Insurance Corporation

MAP-21	Moving Ahead for Progress in the 21st Century Act
PBGC	Pension Benefit Guaranty Corporation
PIMS	Pension Insurance Modeling System
PPA	Pension Protection Act of 2006
PPF	Pension Protection Fund
UK	United Kingdom

November 7, 2012
The Honorable Tom Harkin
Chairman
Committee on Health, Education, Labor,
and Pensions United States Senate

Dear Mr. Chairman:

The Pension Benefit Guaranty Corporation (PBGC) is a government corporation established under the Employee Retirement Income Security Act of 1974 (ERISA)[1] to protect the pension benefits of American workers. As of the end of fiscal year 2011, PBGC was responsible for insuring the benefits of nearly 44 million workers, retirees, and beneficiaries participating in about 27,000 private sector defined benefit (DB) plans, but faced an accumulated deficit of $26 billion. The bulk of this deficit ($23 billion) is attributable to PBGC's single-employer program,[2] reflecting the disparity between the value of future benefits owed to participants of terminated plans insured under this program and the funds available to pay for these benefits. PBGC's deficit has increased over the last decade—mostly due to the termination of a few large, underfunded single-employer DB plans, as well as investment losses and declines in interest rates following the economic downturn. At the same time, PBGC's financial condition has been adversely affected by long-standing structural challenges—including a steady decline in the number of private employers sponsoring DB plans and a statutory premium structure that does not adequately reflect the risk of future claims from plan terminations.[3]

Congress has periodically increased premium rates for plan sponsors within the current premium structure to help put the agency on a firmer financial footing, most recently in the Pension Protection Act of 2006 (PPA)[4] and the Moving Ahead for Progress in the 21st Century Act (MAP-21), enacted July 6, 2012.[5] Nevertheless, PBGC still faces a substantial deficit from past claims and exposure to risk of losses from future claims that could potentially lead to the agency's insolvency.

One proposal to help address the agency's deficit—specified in the President's fiscal year 2013 budget—would give PBGC the authority to move to a more risk-based premium structure for plan sponsors participating in the single-employer program. To gain a better understanding of the advantages and disadvantages of such a proposal, you asked us to examine (1) the options that are available to adjust premiums to improve PBGC's long-term financial condition, (2) the potential implications of these options for plan sponsors and participants, and (3) the potential implementation challenges in moving to a risk-based premium structure.

To determine what options are available to adjust PBGC's premium structure to improve its future financial condition, we first reviewed relevant federal laws pertaining to PBGC's current premiums, including increases to premiums made under MAP-21 (see app. I), and PBGC policies for collecting premiums for the single-employer program. We then reviewed the President's proposal for more risk-based premiums (see app. II), as well as various academic and policy papers that suggest other approaches that might be considered in redesigning PBGC's premium structure. We also obtained data from a model PBGC developed to illustrate different premium options. We assessed the validity of the model's formulas and assessed the reliability of the model's data set of 2,699 plans. We used the model's data set, which represented 81 percent of the DB population in plan year 2010, to conduct further analyses of various options (see app. III). In addition, we interviewed PBGC officials and other federal officials from the Department of Commerce, Federal Deposit Insurance Corporation (FDIC), the Department of Labor (Labor), and the Department of the Treasury about these options, as well as pension officials from the United Kingdom's (UK) Pension Protection Fund (PPF)—an agency that provides benefit insurance to participants in DB plans and charges risk-based premiums to plans sponsors in the UK (see app. IV).[6] To better understand how PBGC determines its risk exposure for future claims and losses, we obtained information about how PBGC calculates its deficit (see app. V) and how PBGC uses the Pension Insurance Modeling System (PIMS), one of the modeling tools the agency uses to make estimates of its future financial condition and evaluate premium options (see app. VI). While PBGC's Inspector General found problems with some detailed data generated by PIMS,[7] we reviewed the PIMS data provided to us and conducted a meeting with PBGC officials to discuss the reliability of these data. We determined that the PIMS data provided to us and used by PBGC in its 2010 exposure report[8] were sufficiently reliable to provide information on the approximate magnitude of PBGC's future financial condition and to generally understand the mechanics of premium options.

To obtain information about the potential implications of different premium options for plan sponsors and participants and the potential implementation challenges of moving to a risk-based premium structure, we interviewed a small judgmental sample of nine plan sponsors, selected to reflect an array of characteristics including plan size, sponsor financial condition, and union involvement. We also conducted interviews with a broad range of pension experts including academics, actuaries, business organizations, and labor officials. (See app. VII for a list of plan sponsors and organizations we contacted.)

We conducted this performance audit between July 2011 and November 2012 in accordance with generally accepted government auditing standards. Those standards require that we plan and perform the audit to obtain sufficient, appropriate evidence to provide a reasonable basis for our findings and conclusions based on our audit objectives. We believe the evidence obtained provides a reasonable basis for our findings and conclusions based on our audit objectives.

BACKGROUND

PBGC was established under ERISA, in part, to insure the pension benefits of participants in qualified DB plans and pay participants up to certain statutory limits should their plans be terminated with insufficient funds.[9] DB plans provide a benefit that is determined by a formula based on various factors specified in the plan, such as an employee's salary, years of service, and age at retirement.

PBGC has a three-member board of directors, consisting of the Secretaries of the Departments of Commerce, Labor, and the Treasury, that is charged with providing policy direction and oversight of PBGC's finances and operations. PBGC's Director is appointed by the President and subject to Senate confirmation. 10 Consistent with our previous recommendations concerning challenges to PBGC's governance,[11] the recently enacted MAP-21 included numerous provisions to strengthen PBGC's board and governance structure overall (see app. I).[12]

PBGC administers two separate insurance programs: a single-employer program and a multiemployer program[13] and is charged with encouraging continuation of private pension plans, providing for timely and uninterrupted payment of participants' pension benefits (up to the insured limits) should plans be terminated with insufficient funds, and maintaining premiums established under the statute at the lowest level consistent with its obligations under ERISA.[14] PBGC-insured DB plans have been in decline since the 1980s. As of 2011, PBGC insured about 25,500 single-employer DB plans covering about 34 million participants, down from nearly 92,000 plans in 1990. During this period, many sponsors have voluntarily terminated their plans as "standard" terminations. Standard terminations occur when sponsors terminate fully funded plans by purchasing a group annuity contract from an insurance company, under which the insurance company agrees to pay all accrued benefits, or by paying lump-sum benefits to participants if permissible.[15] An event preceding at least some of these terminations was a so-called plan "freeze"—an amendment to the plan to limit some or all future pension accruals for some or all plan participants.[16]

PBGC Funding and Deficit

To finance its operations, PBGC has three key sources of funds: (1) pension assets obtained from underfunded, terminated single-employer plans which it takes over;[17] (2) premiums paid by both single-employer and multiemployer plan sponsors; and (3) investment income and net gains and losses generated from the investment of these funds.[18] Figure 1 shows that the annual amount of PBGC's new claims in the single-employer program has fluctuated dramatically during the last 12 years— sometimes exceeding the amount of premiums and thereby contributing to persistent deficits.[19] In contrast, as illustrated in figure 1, the amount of premium revenue PBGC has collected from plans in the single-employer program has been much less volatile, growing fairly steadily over the last 10 years from $967 million in fiscal year 2002 (adjusted for inflation) to nearly $2.1 billion in fiscal year 2011.

As of the end of fiscal year 2011, PBGC's single-employer program had an accumulated deficit of just over $23 billion, which is the result of comparing the value of its assets with the value of its liabilities for claims incurred to date.[20] Although there are differing views about the appropriateness of the assumptions PBGC uses in calculating its deficit,[21] there is general agreement that failure to address various structural challenges could have consequences for both PBGC's long-term financial condition and the health of the DB system. Market performance and low interest rates affect

PBGC's financial position, but so, too, have various structural challenges, including historically inadequate plan funding requirements and premium levels for private DB plan sponsors. To help address these structural challenges, PPA attempted to strengthen plan funding requirements, but these changes were modified or postponed due to the economic downturn, resulting in reduced funding for plans. In addition, MAP-21 included provisions to increase premium rates effective beginning in 2013, but left the current premium structure intact.

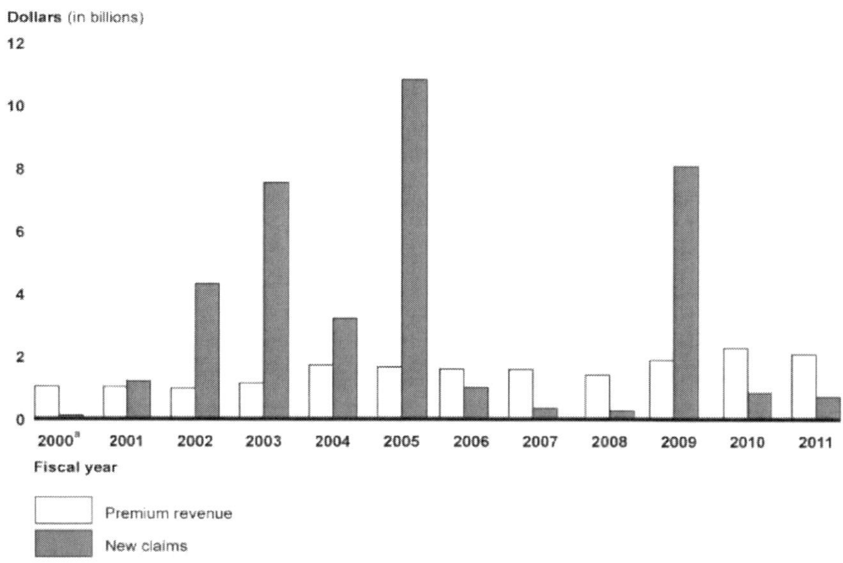

Source: GAO analysis of PBGC data.
Note: Data adjusted for inflation.
[a]New claims for fiscal year 2000 were $110 million.

Figure 1. PBGC's Annual Premium Revenue Compared to New Claims for the Single-Employer Program, Fiscal Years 2000-2011.

PBGC has reported a net accumulated deficit since 2002. As a result of these deficits and structural issues impeding PBGC's ability to adequately fund its insurance programs, including the likelihood of large, unfunded pension plan terminations, we have designated PBGC's single-employer program as high risk since 2003. 22 PBGC receives no funds from general tax revenue. However, if at some point in the future the agency were to exhaust all of its assets and become insolvent, its commitments would not be backed by the full faith and credit of the federal government,[23] and the agency would only have premium revenue to rely on to pay its benefit obligations. As a consequence, PBGC could be forced to dramatically cut benefit payments to participants, seek federal assistance, or raise premiums significantly to meet its benefit commitments. In previous reports on PBGC, we have recommended that PBGC's premium structure be re-examined to explore whether premiums could better reflect the risk posed by various plans to the pension system.[24]

What Could Happen Should PBGC's Single-Employer Program Become Insolvent

Because PBGC would be unable to fully pay benefit obligations to its insured participants, the insolvency of PBGC's single-employer program would potentially threaten the retirement security of millions of Americans. Insolvency implies that PBGC's insurance programs will have exhausted all assets on hand used to pay benefit obligations to its insured participants. If that were to occur, PBGC could no longer rely on investment income from these assets or the value of the assets themselves to pay these benefits. PBGC would thus become entirely dependent on its premium revenue stream to pay benefit obligations. Had insolvency occurred in 2011, PBGC would have been unable to pay all benefits obligated to participants using only premium revenues. That year, PBGC paid nearly $5.5 billion in benefits but only collected $2.1 billion in premium income. The last year that PBGC's premium revenue exceeded the amounts of benefits paid was 1999, when PBGC collected $902 million in premiums and paid $901 million in benefits.

PBGC's Current Premium Structure

Under the current premium structure for its single-employer program, PBGC collects from sponsors a per participant flat-rate premium and a variable-rate premium that is based on a plan's level of underfunding.[25] PBGC also collects a termination premium from sponsors of single-employer plans that terminate their plans under certain criteria.[26] While conceptually, PBGC uses the flat-rate premium as a proxy for exposure based on the number of participants, to the extent that the premium structure relies on flat-rate premiums, sponsors with greater numbers of participants pay more toward the cost of covering risk than sponsors with smaller numbers of participants, regardless of the ages of the participants, the average level of plan benefits, or other risk-related differences. To the extent that the premium structure relies on variable-rate premiums, sponsors with more underfunded plans pay more toward the cost of covering risk than sponsors with better funded plans, regardless of the riskiness of the plan assets or the financial health of the plan sponsor. As a result, there is concern that the current statutory premium structure does not allocate premiums to match the variation in risk posed by different plan sponsors. In fact, the heavy focus on the flat-rate premium tends to create a cross-subsidy paid by financially healthy sponsors to cover the risks posed by sponsors that are less financially strong. For plan years beginning in 2006, the base flat rate was $30 per participant, increasing with inflation adjustments to $35 for 2012, while the base variable rate remained at $9 for every $1,000 of plan underfunding. Under provisions enacted in MAP-21, rates were increased within this same premium structure. The flat-rate premium begins to rise in 2013, and then the variable-rate premium begins to rise in 2014. Beginning in 2013, the variable-rate premium is also subject to a $400 per participant limit (see table 1).[27]

Table 1. Premium Rates under MAP-21

			Rates by plan year		
Rate type	2011	2012	2013	2014	2015
Flat rate (per participant)	$35[a]	$35[a]	$42	$49	$49 or more based on indexing[b]
Variable rate (per $1,000 of unfunded vested benefits)[c]	$9	$9	$9 or more based on indexing[c]	$13 or more based on indexing[c]	$18 or more based on indexing[c]

Sources: MAP-21, Pub. L. No. 112-141, § 40221, 126 Stat. 405, 850-52.

[a] This reflects the base rate of $30 adjusted for inflation.

[b] After 2014, rates will be indexed based on increases in the national average wage index, as determined by the Social Security Administration, and then rounded to the nearest whole dollar.

[c] Though calculated based on the amount of underfunding, the variable rate is subject to a per participant limit of $400 for 2013, with indexing based on increases in the national average wage index, as determined by the Social Security Administration. In addition, MAP-21 provided for an additional $4 increase in plan year 2014, plus an additional $5 increase in plan year 2015.

Historical Premium Rates Have Been Inadequate to Cover Claims

Historically, PBGC's premiums have not fully reflected the risks PBGC insures against—chiefly that a plan sponsor with an underfunded plan will become bankrupt, forcing the termination of the plan and imposing a claim on PBGC.[28] Risks related to potential new claims depend largely on plan sponsor behavior, while PBGC's risks post-termination depend largely on the agency's own investment strategy, among other things (see table 2).

Table 2. PBGC's Risk Exposure

Type of risk	Description
New claims risk	PBGC exposure is based on several factors: • plan sponsor behavior with regard to maintaining plans, funding plans, and investment strategy(allocation of plan assets) • size of new claims • economic conditions, including the level of bankruptcies, market returns, and interest rates • adequacy of premium levels, either set by Congress or by PBGC if granted such authority • impact of plan freezes • deterioration in performance of particular industries • participant longevity improvements greater than expected
PBGC financial risk	PBGC exposure is based on several factors: • PBGC's investment strategy • market returns and interest rate movements • participant longevity improvements greater than expected

Source: GAO analysis of PBGC's 2010 exposure report.

PBGC has estimated that if premium rates were kept at fiscal year 2011 levels,[29] total premium revenue from single-employer plans over the next 10 years would be less than the amount of expected new claims. In addition, many pension experts and the administration believe that PBGC premiums have been much lower than what a private financial institution would charge for insuring the same risk and are insufficient for PBGC to meet its long-term obligations. Indeed, one study estimated that the overall premiums collected by PBGC are equal to about 50 percent of what a private insurer would charge because its premiums do not adequately account for risks.[30] To set premiums at a level sufficient to cover PBGC's total risk exposure would require an analysis of total risk. Several methods have been used to estimate PBGC's total risk exposure with widely varying results, as described in table 3.

Table 3. Various Estimates of PBGC's Total Risk Exposure

Estimation method	Description
Credit ratings of sponsors with underfunded plans	Estimate risk exposure from underfunding by plan sponsors whose credit ratings are below investment grade or that meet one or more financial distress criteria. PBGC already performs this analysis by classifying these sponsors' underfunded plans as reasonably possible terminations.
Market value of insurance	Estimate risk exposure from the price a private insurer would charge. In a 2005 report, the Congressional Budget Office (CBO) estimated PBGC's risk exposure using this method based on the price that a private insurer would charge to accept the insurance obligations of PBGC forall plans that terminate over a given time period.
Total unfunded liabilities	Estimate PBGC's risk exposure by calculating the agency's total potential liabilities from underfunding in all PBGC-insured plans, whether these unfunded liabilities are vested or not, and estimate the risk associated with those liabilities.

Source: GAO analysis of reports and data related to PBGC's total risk exposure.

Each method provides quantifiable insight into the extent of PBGC's risk exposure. For example, in fiscal year 2011, PBGC estimated that its risk exposure to reasonably possible terminations in its single-employer program totaled approximately $227 billion, an increase from $170 billion the previous year. Further, PBGC estimated that the total unfunded liabilities in all PBGC-insured plans were $415 billion in fiscal year 2010.[31] CBO estimated that in 2005, the present value of PBGC's net costs for DB pension insurance for single-employer plans over 10 years was about $87 billion. Total costs for the insurance for 15- and 20-year time horizons were $119 billion and $142 billion, respectively.[32] In addition, the CBO has proffered several methods for establishing the target level of premium revenue to be generated. One possibility is to adopt what CBO describes as an "actuarially fair premium structure"— that is, one that would equate the present value of expected premium revenues with the present value of expected costs to PBGC. Notably, based on CBO's 2005 analysis, a uniform risk premium—one that increases both the flat- and variable-rate portions of current-law premiums by a fixed proportion[33]—would yield premium charges that were 6.5 times larger than rates in effect in 2005, with a flat rate of $123.50 per participant per year and a variable rate of $58.50 per $1,000 of underfunding. This increase would have made rates comparable to premiums charged in a private insurance market to cover PBGC's insurance obligations at that time.

VARIOUS OPTIONS ARE AVAILABLE FOR MORE RISK-BASED PREMIUMS

Various options are available to make PBGC's statutory premium structure more risk-based to better reflect the risk of future claims and improve PBGC's financial condition. The variable-rate component of the premium reflects plan and sponsor risk to some extent, but has been based solely on just one risk factor, plan underfunding. There are numerous options available for incorporating additional risk factors into the variable rate to account for greater levels of risk posed to PBGC by certain plans and sponsors, as is done by other insurance agencies in the United States and abroad. For example, the FDIC, which provides deposits insurance, has used a risk-based premium system since 1993. In addition, the UK's pension insurer determines its premiums based on a risk factor for a plan's asset investment mix, as well as the sponsor's financial strength.

Adjusting Premiums within the Current Structure

Even within the current structure, rates could be adjusted to become more risk-based and help PBGC to increase its revenues. Historically, the bulk of premium revenue has been generated from the flat-rate component of the premium (tied to the number of plan participants) that assesses rates equally per capita across all sponsors regardless of risk, rather than the variable-rate component that reflects risk based on level of plan underfunding. By increasing the proportion of revenues generated from the variable rate and increasing rates overall—such as provided under MAP-21[34]—higher premium costs are shifted more to sponsors with plans that are more underfunded (see table 4). Such changes, even under the current structure, make premiums more risk-based than in the past, and could help reduce the growth of PBGC's deficit while providing greater incentive to sponsors to fully fund their plans.

Table 4. Rates under MAP-21 Compared to a Hypothetical Option to Adjust PBGC Premiums under the Current Structure

Premium option	Flat rate per participant	Variable rate per $1000 of plan underfunding	Description
New premium structure provided for in the Moving Ahead for Progress in the 21st Century Act[a]	$49 by plan year 2014 indexed thereafter	$18 by plan year 2015 indexed thereafter	• Phase-in of rate increase • Revenue estimated over 10 years • The variable rate is limited to $400 per participant for plan year 2013 with indexing thereafter • $9 billion in additional premium revenue generated[b] •58% of additional premium revenue attributable to increase in flat rate •42% of additional premium revenue attributable to increase in variable rate
Option to increase rates under the current structure[c]	Flat rate increased so that the increase to total premium revenue is evenly distributed between the flat rate and variable rate	Variable rate increased so that the increase to total premium revenue is evenly distributed between the flat rate and variable rate	•No phase-in of rate increase •Revenue estimated on annual basis over 8 years •$16 billion in additional premium revenue generated ($2billion annually)[d] •50% of additional premium revenue attributable to the flat rate •50% of additional premium revenue attributable to the variable rate

Source: GAO analysis of documents related to PBGC premiums.
[a] MAP-21, § 40221, 126 Stat. 405, 850-852 (2012).
[b] Revenue increase compared to plan year 2012 rates.
[c] For this option, rates were generated by PBGC using a hypothetical model created to explore the effects of different premium options on rates and premium revenue. PBGC's hypothetical model used plan year 2010 data from PBGC's premium database and did not incorporate any projections about future levels of plan funding or participant counts. This hypothetical option increases rates within the current premium structure without incorporating additional risk factors.
[d] Revenue increase compared with estimates under plan year 2010 rates.

To explore this option, PBGC developed a model to illustrate the various ways premiums could be adjusted to meet different revenue targets over varying lengths of time by increasing either the flat rate or the variable rate, or both, by certain percentages.[35] The model used standard quantitative techniques to show how different premium options would affect rates and generate premium revenue over time without a rate phase-in. PBGC officials stressed that the model did not use PIMS for its calculations, and that the model is purely hypothetical and not intended as a policy proposal. However, by way of illustration, PBGC used the model to generate one scenario whereby the additional revenue would be obtained in equal amounts from increases in both the flat and variable rates over 8 years to meet the administration's proposed $16 billion premium revenue target. Under this scenario, PBGC estimated that to reach the annual $2 billion revenue target in the first year without a rate phase-in, premium revenue from both the flat rate and variable rate would have to increase by 77 and 76 percent, respectively. We estimated that under this option, the flat rate would increase to $62 per participant and the variable rate to nearly $16 per $1,000 of plan underfunding.[36] Under this option, 50 percent of the premium revenue increase is attributable to the variable rate compared to 42 percent under MAP-21 rates. However, the only risk factor incorporated into the variable rate under both MAP-21 and PBGC's model scenario described above is plan underfunding, and as discussed further below, PBGC has concluded from its analyses that plan underfunding is a poor proxy for the risk of a new claim.

Alternative Options to Incorporate Additional Risk Factors into Premiums

Other premium options could more fully take into account the agency's exposure to the risk of new claims by incorporating other risk factors. Specifically, PBGC's risk could be better mitigated through alternative premium options that incorporate other risk factors into the variable rate to more fully take into account the agency's exposure to the risk of future losses. Because the variable-rate premium is currently based solely on plan underfunding, it does not capture the agency's overall risk as well as it could if additional risk factors were also taken into consideration, such as a plan's investment strategies, benefit structure and benefit level, demographic profile, or the plan sponsor's financial strength.[37] With congressional action, these additional risk factors could be incorporated into PBGC's rates, providing proportionally greater amounts of revenue from plan sponsors posing greater risk to the agency, and better alignment with the continuum of risk facing the agency.

PBGC has conducted analyses showing that measures of underfunding are poor predictors of plan termination. In these analyses, PBGC reviewed funding levels for plans that had terminated from fiscal years 2009 to 2011, [38] and found the average termination funding level was about 54 percent on the date of termination. For the year previous to termination, the average funding level measurement on which the variable-rate premium was calculated for these plans was about 84 percent. Because of the differences found in a plan's funding-level measurements, PBGC officials believe that measures of a sponsor's financial strength—determined using credit scores or Dun & Bradstreet scores—are better predictors of whether plans terminate than are measures of underfunding.

Much like premiums set by insurance companies, 39 PBGC premium rates could be set based on individual risk profiles for sponsors and their plans. Such incorporation of additional risk factors into premiums could help PBGC to better manage risk by raising proportionally greater amounts of revenue from financially riskier sponsors whose plans are underfunded, and provide an incentive to sponsors to fully fund their plans and reduce other risk factors under their control, such as through less risky plan asset allocation. In addition, as with any premium structure, risk-based premiums could be designed to address only the risk of new costs that PBGC will incur from future claims, or they could be designed to help address PBGC's risk of future insolvency, which also reflects deficit costs from past terminations. Possible approaches for incorporating additional risk factors into PBGC's premium structure are described further below, along with information on the approach used by the FDIC for banking institutions and by PPF for pension plans in the UK (see table 5).

Table 5. Different Options to Incorporate Additional Risk Factors into Premiums

Premium option	Flat rate	Variable rate with additional risk factors	Description
Option to incorporate additional risk factor for sponsor financial health[a]	$44 per participant	Variable rate incorporates additional risk factor for sponsor financial health	• No phase-in of rate increase • Variable rate calculated on a per participant basis • Rates capped at four times plan year 2010 rates on a per participant basis • Revenue estimated on annual basis over 8 years

Premium option	Flat rate	Variable rate with additional risk factors	Description
			• $16 billion in additional premium revenue generated ($2 billion annually)[b] • 16% of additional premium revenue attributable tothe flat rate[c] • 84% of additional premium revenue attributable tothe variable rate[d]
Option to use different methods to calculate premiums based on size of institution (FDIC)	Not applicable	Risk premium incorporates risk factors for size and financial strength	• Different methods used to calculate premiums based on the size of the institution • Premiums are generally set based on a bank's aggregate assets (funding level) and supervisory rating (financial strength) • Premiums based on bank placement into one of four risk categories • Premiums range set to meet annual revenue target needed to insure against identified risk • Premium rates can change quarterly through monitoring of bank capitalization and supervisory data
Option to incorporate additional risk factor for plan investment strategy (UK's PPF)	Plan-based premium (comparable to PBGC flat- rate premium) targeted to meet revenue estimate	Risk-based premium (comparable to PBGC variable- rate premium) incorporates risk factors for plan underfunding, sponsor insolvency, and plan asset investment risk	• Both a plan-based (flat) and risk-based premium charged to sponsors • Premium rates set for 3 years • Scaling factor used to adjust risk-based premiums to meet 3-year revenue target • 10% of premium revenue attributable to plan-based premium and 90% attributable to risk-basedpremium • Smoothing techniques used to adjust premium rates to account for adverse economic conditions

Source: GAO analysis of documents related to PBGC, FDIC, and PPF premiums.

[a] For this option, rates were generated by PBGC using a hypothetical model created to explore the effects of different premium options on rates and premium revenue. PBGC's hypothetical model used plan year 2010 data from PBGC's premium database and did not incorporate any projections about future levels of plan funding or participant counts.

[b] Revenue increase compared with estimates under plan year 2010 rates.

[c] These percentages are for revenue increases attributable to the flat and variable rate before applying the President's proposed cap of four times the per participant rate for plan year 2010.

[d] PPF refers to plans as schemes and premiums as levies. For the purpose of this report, we continue to use plans and premiums when discussing PPF's premium framework.

Modeling More Risk-Based Options under the President's Proposal

The President's 2013 budget proposes to reform how PBGC premiums are determined by giving the PBGC board the authority to take into account the risks that different sponsors pose to their retirees and to PBGC. The President's budget proposes raising $16 billion in additional premium revenue over a 10-year period, from 2013 to 2022, and would require a year of study and public comment before any implementation and the gradual phasing in of any increases due to changes in the premium structure. To reach this target over this period, the administration proposed limiting the premium increase to $4 billion in additional flat-rate premiums and $12 billion in additional variable-rate premiums. By way of comparison, the increases under MAP-21 are estimated to generate $5.1 billion from the flat rate and $3.8 billion from the variable rate over the same period. By relying more heavily on variable-rate premiums than under MAP-21, the President's proposal would result in sponsors posing greater risk to PBGC paying higher premiums, and sponsors posing less risk to PBGC paying lower premiums.

PBGC used its model to explore one possible approach to incorporating an additional risk factor into the variable-rate premium and illustrate how the mechanics of a more risk-based option might work. Under this option, the financial health of a plan sponsor would be taken into account in tandem with the funded level of a plan to enhance the extent to which risk is accounted for in the premium structure. To accomplish this, PBGC calculated the variable-rate premium for each plan based on a combination of both plan underfunding and sponsor financial health, to meet the President's $16 billion premium revenue target. For the financial health factor, PBGC assigned a measure on a scale of 1 to 5 based on the lower of the sponsor's Standard & Poor's or Moody's credit ratings, or, if credit ratings were unavailable, a sponsor's Dun & Bradstreet credit risk ranking. PBGC then combined these scores with scores based on the plan's level of funding to assign a corresponding variable rate used for calculating the premium.

In developing this hypothetical risk-based option, PBGC set rates to reach the $16 billion target over 8 years by raising an additional $2 billion in premium revenue over plan year 2010 premiums without a phase-in period. To accomplish this, PBGC constructed a scenario whereby the flat rate would increase from $35 to $44 per participant, and the variable rate would increase on a per participant basis rather than on the dollar amount of plan underfunding. Specifically, PBGC weighted the variable rate on a sliding scale that increased as plan funding weakened and decreased with stronger financial health of the sponsor (see table 6). The flat and variable rates were combined into a single rate and then capped on a per participant basis, as under the President's proposal, so that the result would not be more than four times the premium rates in plan year 2010.[40] (See appendix III for additional GAO analyses of this premium option.)

Table 6. Total Premium Rates per Participant (Flat + Variable) under a Hypothetical Risk-Based Option

		Funded status		
	(1)	(2)	(3)	(4)
Financial health	**≥120% funded**	**≥90 to under 120% funded**	**75% to under 90% funded**	**<75% funded**
Extremely healthy (1)	$44	$44	$69	$94
Very healthy (2)	$44	$44	$94	$144
Healthy (3)	$74	$104	$119	$194
Risky (4)	$124	$204	$244	$444
Very risky (5)	$134	$224	$269	$494

Source: PBGC.

However, PBGC's estimates under the risk-based option could be adjusted in various ways. For example, the premium rates shown in table 6 that are used in the model could be changed based on the same underfunding and financial strength risk factors, but using different weights. Any combination of weighting could be applied to test different policy options—for example, greater weight could be placed on the rate for financial weakness. The model's rates could be set to track with the actual risk of new claims based on an analysis of historical funding and financial health data correlated with actual claim patterns. In each case, rates would vary for certain sponsors who pose greater risk to PBGC based on financial health.

The risk-based option could also be adjusted to take into account other risk factors associated with different plans' asset investment mixes, the size of a plan relative to the size of its sponsor, and the level of plan benefits and demographic profile of plan participants,[41] as well as to take into account changes in assumptions over time. As with the hypothetical option to increase rates under the current structure, the rates generated by the model under the risk-based option are based on plan year 2010 plan funding and participant counts, and do not include any phase-in of rates or changes to assumptions to reflect changes that may occur over time. Thus, to further fine tune the distribution of the combined underfunding and financial health scores and the associated premium rates, PBGC could incorporate these other risk factors into the model, and change funding and participant count assumptions to allow a rate phase-in. While acknowledging these possibilities, PBGC officials emphasized that the purpose of generating this option was purely to illustrate one hypothetical scenario of how rates could be redesigned to incorporate the additional risk factor of a sponsor's financial health to raise additional premium revenue and to distribute premiums more in line with the risk posed by different plan sponsors—it is not a policy proposal, and the agency has no plans at this time to conduct further analyses to incorporate additional risk factors.

FDIC's Risk-Based Premiums

FDIC, a federal corporation that insures the deposits of all federally insured depository institutions, has long used risk-based premiums to help insure depositors against the risk of loss. In 1993, FDIC adopted a risk-related premium system, which was designed to reduce the cross-subsidy that stronger banks implicitly provided to weaker banks under its previous flat-rate premium system. The new system was intended to provide proper incentives for risk taking, whereby banks who pose a higher risk have a higher premium rate. Under FDIC's risk-based premium system, banks are first categorized on two factors: aggregate assets and a composite supervisory rating reflecting capital, asset quality, management, earnings, liquidity, and sensitivity to market risk (referred to as "CAMELS").[42] FDIC sets assessment (premium) rates to achieve a target "designated reserve ratio" based on the ratio of the deposit insurance fund to insured deposits.[43] Most banks—specifically, those under $10 billion in assets—are placed in four risk categories on the basis of their capital (which is roughly equivalent to a bank's funding level) and CAMELS rating (which is roughly equivalent to a bank's financial health). Following the economic crisis of 2008, FDIC began to reconsider risk- based pricing methods for large banks, taking into account the risks that caused severe problems for large banks. Effective in the second quarter of 2011, FDIC began using different methodologies to set assessment rates for small and large banks. Both systems attempt to have riskier banks pay higher premiums at the time they assume the risk rather than waiting until conditions deteriorate. However, the FDIC charges a higher premium rate for large banks with high asset concentrations and less stable balance sheet liquidity.

The UK's DB Premium Framework

At least one country has already moved to a more risk-based system for determining premium rates. The UK's Pension Protection Fund (PPF)— the government corporation responsible for insuring benefits to participants of DB plans—incorporates additional risk factors into its premium structure.[44] PPF's premium structure has two components: a risk-based premium and a plan-based premium.[45] The risk-based premium is based on the likelihood of a plan making a claim on PPF (which PPF terms "insolvency risk") and the potential size of that claim (which PPF terms "underfunding risk"). PPF uses the Dun & Bradstreet failure score—a measure of the likelihood of sponsor bankruptcy—as the risk factor for determining a sponsor's insolvency risk.[46] PPF uses information about the value of plan assets and liabilities, supplied to the agency by sponsors through an exchange, to calculate a sponsor's underfunding risk.[47] Beginning with plan year 2012/13, PPF will also consider a plan's investment strategy to adjust underfunding risk when calculating a plan's premium. (See appendix IV for a description of the components of PPF's premium formula.) PPF then uses a premium scaling factor to calculate a plan's premium to meet a certain revenue target.[48] The changes adopted for plan year 2012/2013 affect how PPF will calculate both the risk-based premium and the plan-based premium. For example, before these changes, for plan year 2011/12, all sponsors with plans funded up to 155 percent paid a risk-based premium based on an underfunding risk factor that decreased as a plan's funding level increased. Sponsors whose plans were funded at or above 155 percent did not pay a risk-based premium. For the 2012/13 plan year, plan underfunding will be calculated using 5-year financial market indexes—referred to as smoothing[49]—for plan assets and liabilities, and will for the first time take a plan's investment strategy into account, adjusting a plan's underfunding risk based on the plan's level of investment risk. The risk-based premium is also capped to protect the most vulnerable plans.[50] In addition, prior to the 2012/13 plan year, the plan-based premium was based on a plan's estimated liabilities to its participants. Starting with the 2012/13 plan year, the plan-based premium will be based on a plan's smoothed liabilities to its participants and on a premium multiplier to cover the costs to the agency of capping the highest risk-based premiums. As a result, the plan-based premium will account for a smaller percentage of the total premium, decreasing its portion of the total premium from 20 percent to an estimated 10 percent.[51] Beyond these basics, PPF's premium framework differs from PBGC's current premium structure and from other proposals to redesign PBGC premiums in a number of more subtle ways as well. Key features include the following:

- *Equitable basis of PPF's plan-based levy.* The plan-based premium used prior to the 2012/13 plan year can be considered, essentially, PPF's version of PBGC's flat-rate premium. The difference is that PBGC's flat-rate premium is calculated on a per participant basis, whereas PPF's plan-based premium is a percentage of the liability owed to participants. The percentage of liability approach is a more equitable distribution in the sense that it is based on the total liability owed by a plan to its participants, rather than on a plan's participant count (a plan could have many participants but a relatively small liability, or few participants but a very large liability, so that the number of participants *per se* has limitations as a measure of exposure). For example, consider two plans with the same number of participants, but one has a liability twice as large as the other (either because of more generous benefits or costlier demographics). Although, all other things being equal, the plan with greater liability is riskier, under its current premium structure, PBGC would charge both plans the same fixed premium, whereas PPF would have charged a larger plan-based premium to the plan with greater liabilities.
- *Proportionality in PPF's underfunding factor.* In the risk-based premium option modeled by PBGC, a plan's funded status is represented by its funded ratio (the ratio of plan assets to plan liabilities). The variable rate applied to that plan is, in part, determined using that ratio to assign the sponsor to one of the designated risk premium categories and the rate is then applied on a per participant basis. In contrast, PPF represents funded status by the actual financial value of the unfunded liability of each plan and does not assign a plan to a funded category, but instead applies a premium directly to the unfunded amount (similar to the current PBGC variable-rate premium), so that the premium charged is more proportional to the individual unfunded exposure of the plan. By being directly linked to the level of underfunding in each individual plan, PPF's premium may more accurately reflect the level of risk posed by plans than the hypothetical approach modeled by PBGC.
- *Linkage of PPF premiums to long-term funding strategy.* PPF publishes a long-term funding strategy, which sets out how the agency intends to have the financial resources needed to pay existing levels of compensation to current and future PPF participants and become financially self-sufficient by 2030.[52] Integral to its funding strategy, PPF monitors how its premiums might need to change under different

economic circumstances in order to meet its funding target.[53] Although PBGC publishes an annual exposure report—which estimates future claims and premium revenues—it does not currently have the statutory authority to change rates based on these estimates to meet specific revenue targets.

- *Proportionality and effectiveness of including plan asset allocation as a risk factor.* Although new for PPF and therefore untested, incorporating this significant risk factor into rates could better align premiums with risk and could also provide an incentive for sponsors to use less risky asset allocations.

In addition, there are differences related to risk premium caps between PPF's framework and PBGC's proposed risk-based premium that could potentially have distributional effects on rates and premium levels. The cap on PPF's risk-based premium is 75 basis points (0.75 percent) of the plan's liability to its participants. This compares to the administration's proposal for a different type of cap for PBGC whereby premiums would be limited to four times a sponsor's plan year 2010 premiums on a per participant basis and the new $400 per participant variable-rate limit set by MAP-21. How premium caps are calculated could change the distributional pattern of the amount of premiums sponsors would pay under different premium options, and could adjust the total amount of revenue collected by PBGC under these options.

Moving to a More Risk-Based Structure Shifts Premium Costs to Riskier Sponsors

Compared to the distribution of costs under the current structure, premium costs would be redistributed to those sponsors posing greater risk to PBGC under a more risk-based structure. For example, if the financial health of the plan sponsor were included as a risk factor, financially risky sponsors would pay more, while financially healthy sponsors would pay less. A more risk-based structure such as this would decrease the cross-subsidization present in the current premium structure that relies largely on the flat rate charged to all sponsors based on number of participants no matter the level of risk they pose. Pension experts and plan sponsors we spoke with raised various concerns about this redistribution of costs. For example, some voiced concerns that the higher premiums for some plan sponsors might increase the frequency of plan freezes and terminations; [54] however, our previous work indicates that, generally, this would be unlikely. Some noted that depending on the way risk is incorporated, premiums could rise during recessions when financially weak companies are least able to bear the costs, especially smaller companies. Some also expressed concern about the equity of various premium redesign options, especially those that require current sponsors to pay higher premiums to address PBGC's deficit for prior plan terminations. Experts and officials suggested various ways to address such concerns.

Financially Risky Sponsors Would Be Charged Higher Premiums

Under a more risk-based structure that included sponsor financial health as a risk factor, premium costs would be redistributed to better reflect the risk posed by each plan sponsor. To better understand the implications of moving to one such more risk-based structure, we analyzed the data provided in PBGC's sample of 2,699 plans to determine the range of per participant rates sponsors would pay under PBGC's hypothetical risk-based option compared with rates in plan year 2010 and the increases scheduled to be in place in 2015 as a result of MAP-21. As summarized in table 7, compared with rates in 2010, minimum rates are higher across the board under both the act and the more risk-based option, while the maximum rates are lower due to the adoption of a variable-rate limit (four times the per participant rate paid in plan year 2010 for the hypothetical risk-based option and no more than $400 per participant under MAP-21). In a comparison of rates under the risk-based option with estimated rates under MAP-21 in plan year 2015, those with plans that are well funded (that is, funded at 120 percent or more) could see their rates decrease slightly ($44 vs. $49) if they are financially healthy, while their rates could more than double ($134 vs. $49) if they are categorized as very risky. Among those with plans that are poorly funded (that is, funded at less than 75 percent), sponsors could see higher rates under the more risk-based structure depending on whether they are financially healthy or not ($94 to $494 vs. $57 to $449). For example, a poorly funded plan that is categorized as very risky could see its rates increase as much as $257 per participant. PBGC officials noted, however, that while technically correct, few plans are likely to have variable-rate premiums near these upper-end caps.

Table 7. Hypothetical Risk-Based Option Premium Rates Compared to Rates in Plan Year 2010 and in Plan Year 2015 under MAP-21

Dollars per participant				
	Range of per participant premium rates among plans in sample[a]			
	>120% funded	**>90% to under 120% funded**	**75% to under 90% funded**	**<75% funded**
Plan year 2010 rates[b]	$35	$35-$315	$38-$708	$39-$2,481
Plan year 2015 rates under MAP-21 (estimated)[c]	49	49-449	54-449	57-449
PBGC's hypothetical risk-based option (incorporates additional risk factor for financial health) d	44-134	44-224	69-269	94-494

Source: GAO analysis of PBGC data from a sample of defined benefit plans used in PBGC's hypothetical premium model.

[a] For the most part, PBGC's model used plan year 2010 data from a sample of 2,699 DB plans covering 27.5 million participants. The model covered 81 percent of all PBGC-insured participants (33.8 million) in 2010. However, in some instances, PBGC used 2009 data to calculate per participant rates for sponsors. In those instances, the lower bound of the per participant rate was $34, since the flat rate was $34 per participant in 2009. Thus, we chose to limit our analysis of PBGC's model to data from 2010.

[b] To calculate the per participant rates for plan year 2010, PBGC divided the total premiums each plan paid in plan year 2010 by the participant count for that plan. To calculate the range of premium rates by funding level, we grouped PBGC's per participant rates data for each plan into the four funding categories PBGC used in its hypothetical premiums model.

[c] Pub. L. No. 112-141, 126 Stat. 405 (2012). Rates under MAP-21 for 2015 are estimated using data from PBGC's premium model, including participant and underfunding levels from 2010. We estimated rates by placing a limit of $400 on the variable rate on a per participant basis as required under the act and by grouping per participant rates data for each plan into the four funding categories PBGC used in its hypothetical premiums model.

[d] Rates under this option are affected by both the aggregate funding level for a sponsor's plan and the sponsor's financial health rating. To calculate the per participant rates for the risk-based option, PBGC used plans' funding levels and participant counts from its plan year 2010 premium database and incorporated financial health data for each sponsor. Based on a plan's funding level and the financial health of the plan's sponsor, PBGC assigned each plan to a risk category that carried a specific per participant rate. To calculate the range of premium rates by funding level, we grouped PBGC's per participant rates data for each plan into the four funding categories PBGC used for this option in its hypothetical premiums model.

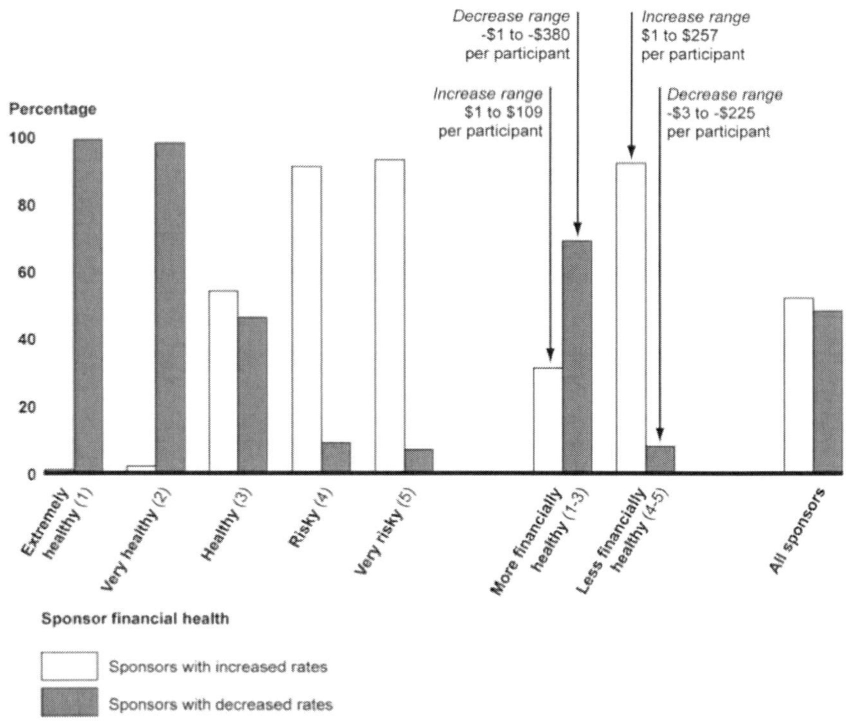

Source: GAO analysis of PBGC data from a sample of 2,699 defined benefit plans used in PBGC's hypothetical premium model.

Figure 2. Percentage of Sample Sponsors with Premium Rate Changes under PBGC's Hypothetical Risk-Based Option Compared with Estimated Rates in Plan Year 2015 under MAP-21.

To determine how these rate changes would be redistributed at the company level, rather than at the plan level, we aggregated the data in PBGC's sample by sponsor. We found that the 2,699 plans in the sample were sponsored by 1,114 different companies. As summarized in figure 2, our analysis suggests that for the two-thirds of companies that were ranked more financially healthy (that is, sponsors whose financial health is considered extremely healthy, very healthy, or healthy), premiums would decrease for a majority (71 percent of sample companies). These decreases were largely due to the lower flat rate under the risk-based option compared to the MAP-21 rate. In contrast, for the companies that were ranked less financially healthy (that is, sponsors whose financial health is considered either risky or very risky), premiums could increase for most (92 percent of these sample companies). The increases were mainly due to how the financial health risk factor affects per participant rates under the risk-based option for these companies, regardless of level of plan underfunding.

Because rates under the risk-based option are calculated on a per participant basis, the magnitude of these changes will vary by company depending on the number of participants in the plan or plans that they sponsor. For example, among the 143 least financially healthy companies with increases in premiums under PBGC's risk-based option, the number of plans and participants for companies varied widely. On the small end of the spectrum, one company sponsored a plan with 825 participants. This company's estimated total premium cost would be $407,550 under PBGC's risk-based premium, compared with $370,425 under MAP-21 in plan year 2015, a 10 percent increase. On the large end, another company sponsored a plan with 327,463 participants. This company's estimated total premium cost would be $100.9 million under PBGC's risk-based premium, compared with $43.2 million under MAP-21 in plan year 2015, a 133 percent increase, even with the cap.

Premium Changes Have Not Been Key Factors in Decisions to Freeze or Terminate Plans

Although plan sponsors and experts expressed varying opinions about how moving to a more risk-based premium structure might influence plan sponsors, our previous work on the subject found that increases in premium costs were not a significant reason for sponsors to freeze or terminate their DB plans. Among the many reasons sponsors cited in our 2008 report for freezing their largest plans, the most often cited were the impact of annual contributions on their firm's cash flows and the unpredictability of plan funding. The factors that were most likely to influence implementing a hard freeze—that is, a freeze that ceases all future benefit accruals—were sponsor size and the extent to which a sponsor's plans are subject to collective bargaining agreements.[55] A more recent survey of DB plan sponsors by Towers Watson reported similar findings.[56] Sponsors cited reducing cost and minimizing cost volatility as the primary reasons for freezing plans or converting plans to some other type of retirement savings instrument. PBGC premium increases were not mentioned by sponsors as a factor for freezing or converting their plans.[57]

Moreover, according to PBGC officials, premiums generally account for a small percentage of compensation costs.[58]

Nevertheless, several experts and others we spoke with pointed out that increased premium costs could have negative implications for DB plan sponsors. For example, some commented that increased premiums might divert funds that sponsors would have otherwise used to fund their pension plans or other company priorities such as job creation and business investment. A few told us they viewed a potential increase in PBGC premiums simply as a tax increase on companies that sponsor DB pension plans. One sponsor we spoke with commented that DB pension plans are already in duress because of historically low interest rates for plan funding obligations, and that increased premium costs would add another challenge to sponsors. Another noted that it is increasingly more difficult to justify the costs of DB pension plans to management, and increased premiums may be the final factor in a sponsors' decision to freeze or terminate their plan. However, another sponsor said that given all the other challenges facing pension plans, increasing premiums is unlikely to have a significant effect.

Pension experts we spoke with also differed in their opinion on whether implementing a new premium structure would lead to plan freezes or terminations. Several—including, five business professionals, three academics, one labor representative, one actuary, and one federal official—noted that increased premium costs may cause an increase in plan freezes or terminations, which could result in negative implications for the retirement security of plan participants.[59] As one academic noted, under a risk-based premium structure, premium costs for financially healthy plans and sponsors may decrease, while financially unhealthy plans and sponsors will likely have increased premium costs, further worsening their financial position and potentially causing these plan sponsors to exit the DB system. However, others stated that they believed that increased premiums will not increase plan freezes and terminations. For example, an agency official said that premiums historically have been set low, and premium increases are unlikely to cause plan freezes or terminations. Additionally, another agency official noted that since there are many factors influencing plan sponsors' decisions to terminate a plan, premium increases will likely have little impact.

Nevertheless, pension plan freezes and terminations have become more common in recent years, weakening the DB system. Plan freezes increased nearly 50 percent from 2003 to 2008. Specifically, PBGC reported that as of the end of 2009, approximately 27 percent of all PBGC-insured plans were hard frozen. 60 Voluntary standard terminations have also increased in recent years, with an approximately 29 percent increase from fiscal year 2003 to 2010.[61] Data provided by PBGC indicate that, from 2000 to 2010, about 1.2 million participants were in plans that ceased to exist because of standard plan terminations.[62] The Towers Watson survey found that approximately two-thirds of sponsors that once offered a DB plan to new hires no longer offer these benefits; however, the survey also found that many active DB sponsors remain committed to offering a DB plan in the future.[63]

Other Potential Behavioral Effects Cited, but Impact Uncertain

Rather than inducing plan sponsors to freeze or terminate their plans, several pension experts—as well as PBGC officials—expressed the hope that moving to a more risk-based premium system would encourage less risky behavior among plan sponsors. For example, when faced with increased premiums for increased risk, sponsors might adopt safer asset allocation practices or contribute more to their plans to keep funding levels higher. In an attempt to quantify this incentive, one pension actuary has noted that the current variable-rate premium can have an economic effect equivalent to an additional return on investment. For example, when, in 2015, the variable rate reaches $18 per year per $1,000 of underfunding, an additional $100 contributed to an underfunded plan will reduce annual premiums by $1.80, or 1.80 percent, and so can be viewed as boosting investment return by almost 2 percent— which is a potentially stronger incentive to fund the plan than what exists currently. Similarly, the new premium assessment in the UK based on the riskiness of plan asset allocation could possibly induce plan sponsors to shift to somewhat less risky asset allocations. Either effect—increased funding or less risky asset allocations—would, in turn, reduce the risk to the pension insurer. Little is yet known about the likelihood or magnitude of these potential effects, however, and PBGC does not include any behavioral impacts in its modeling.

Concerns Raised That Risk-Based Premiums Could Increase during Recessions

Some pension experts we spoke with raised concerns about the potential for premiums to rise when companies are least able to bear the costs, as could be the case during recessions. Depending on how risk factors are incorporated into rates, premiums could have a pro-cyclical effect—that is, they would increase during economic downturns. As economic conditions worsen, more companies would fall into the less financially healthy categories, and more plans would become less well-funded, resulting in higher premiums. This could lead to financially weaker firms being required to pay higher premiums at precisely the time that they can least afford to do so.

However, increases in premiums under the current premium structure are already pro-cyclical. For example, the increases in the variable rate under MAP-21, enacted in July 2012, would cause rates to increase to the extent that plan underfunding increased during a recession when firms are least capable of paying higher premiums. Recognizing that such increased premium costs could prove a hardship for some sponsors, Congress included a cap on premium increases under MAP-21, and the President's proposal also included a cap.[64] Additional steps could be taken to address such concerns with cyclicality under a more risk-based premium structure. For example, PBGC officials said that, in addition to caps, they would consider supporting the use of an average of a sponsor's 5-year funding levels to help smooth the impact that economic cycles would have on risk-based premium rates.[65]

FDIC faced similar concerns when designing its new premium system for financial institutions in 2006. To address these concerns, the FDIC capped premiums for its riskiest category of institutions at 60 percent below what the premium amount would be under a purely risk-based system.[66] In adopting this cap, FDIC sought to address long-standing concerns of the industry, regulators, and others that premiums should not be set so high as to prevent an institution that is troubled and seeking to rebuild its health from doing so. As a result of the cap, however, some degree of cross-subsidy still exists in the premium system between financially healthier institutions and troubled institutions.

The impact of having to pay higher rates under a new premium structure also may pose more of a challenge for some smaller companies than some larger ones, as they may have fewer resources to draw from for these added costs.

The data in PBGC's premium model do not include information on company size, such as a sponsor's assets, revenue, operating costs, or payroll expenditures. Without such data, it is unclear the extent to which smaller companies may experience a greater hardship under the risk-based option compared with larger companies.

However, consideration of company size could be incorporated into a redesigned premium structure. For example, in designing its premium system, the FDIC created a structure that differentiates between large and small institutions. Large institutions are priced using one of two "scorecards"— one for the majority of large institutions, and a separate scorecard for very large institutions that are structurally and operationally complex or that pose unique challenges and risks in case of failure. Each scorecard combines a performance score and a loss severity score.

The scorecard for large and complex institutions incorporates various measures of market risk. Smaller institutions have their premiums based on financial ratios, such as an institution's capital, past-due loans, and income, and its CAMELS ratings. For smaller institutions, FDIC data show that the higher on the CAMELS scale institutions are rated, the higher the rate of failure.

General Concerns about Equity Implications of Increasing Premiums Also Raised

Plan sponsors and others we spoke with also raised some concerns about the equity of increasing premiums under a more risk-based structure. In particular, several raised concerns about having current sponsors pay higher premiums to pay for PBGC's liabilities from plans terminated in the past. Further, the amount of revenue currently being proposed to be raised through increased premiums is unlikely to cover the full amount of future claims, let alone help to address liabilities due to past claims.

These concerns are not unique to a more risk-based premium structure. Increasing rates under the current premium structure also gives rise to concerns about equity implications, and is the reason for adopting premium caps.[67]

However, such provisions do not alleviate the equity concerns of how to deal with "legacy costs" from plans terminated in the past. To further address such equity concerns, several pension experts noted the need to separate PBGC's existing liabilities from the projected cost of future claims, and they suggested various alternative surcharges for accomplishing this goal (see table 8).[68] These surcharges attempt to raise revenue to pay existing liabilities more equitably by targeting companies that have re-emerged from bankruptcy, that are in industries with the largest previous claims, and that are past as well as current sponsors. However, as noted in the table, each has drawbacks that limit its effectiveness as a potential revenue-raising tool for this purpose.

Table 8. Options Suggested by Experts to Address PBGC's Past Deficit Costs

Bankruptcy Re-Emergence Surcharge	A surcharge could be levied against sponsors whose plans terminate in bankruptcy, but re-emerge after turning over their liabilities to PBGC. The surcharge would be separate from, and in addition to, the termination premium, which is levied on plan sponsors that terminate an underfunded pension plan.[a]Such a surcharge could promote greater accountability among plan sponsors responsible for PBGC's deficit, but may place a serious financial burden on these formerly bankrupt companies.
Industry-Specific Surcharge	A surcharge could be levied on those industries that have accounted for a disproportionate amount of PBGC's deficit. For example, the government could impose a fee on airline tickets that would cover the underfunded airline plans that have been taken over by PBGC. This surcharge may incentivize plan sponsors within certain industries to manage their plans more responsibly. However, it may also place a financial burden on these companies or their customers through increased prices,and these companies would not be the same companies that contributed to PBGC's deficit by terminating their plans in the past.
Retirement Sponsor Surcharge	A surcharge could be levied on an ongoing basis across all DB plan participants, and/or a one-time surcharge could be levied on any past or present sponsor that provides a DB retirement plan. This approach recognizes that all DB plan sponsors have a stake in the health of the DB retirement system, and PBGC's insurance program that helps protect its participants. However, this surcharge would place an additional cost on healthy plan sponsors who are less likely to be responsible for contributing to PBGC's deficit by terminating their plans in the future.

Source: GAO interviews with pension experts.

[a]29 U.S.C. 1306(a)(7). Specifically, a termination premium of $1,250 per participant per year for 3 years generally applies when a single-employer plan terminates in a distress termination under 29 U.S.C. § 1341(c)(2)(B)(ii) or (iii) or in an involuntary termination under 29 U.S.C. § 1342. However, this premium does not apply in the case of a plan terminated under 29 U.S.C. §§ 1341(c)(2)(B)(ii) or 1342 during the pendency of a bankruptcy reorganization (29 U.S.C. § 1306(7)(b)), or to any plan termination during the pendency of any bankruptcy reorganization filed before October 18, 2005 (Deficit Reduction Act of 2005, Pub. L. No. 109-171, § 8101(b) and (d), 120 Stat. 181-22 and 183 (2006)).

In addition, some plan sponsors and others we spoke with voiced concerns about whether potential risk-based factors could equitably represent the future risk of particular sponsors and their plans to PBGC or could have other adverse consequences for sponsors. For example, some sponsors expressed concern about including a risk factor measuring plan asset investment mix, in particular, because, as noted by one sponsor, it is important for plan sponsors to invest assets according to their individual needs and priorities. Some experts also expressed equity concerns about the potential inclusion of a creditworthiness factor. One expert stated that if information about the financial status of DB plan sponsors were made public, it could put these companies at a competitive disadvantage compared to companies that do not sponsor DB plans.[69] A few plan sponsors said that risk-based premiums are conceptually appealing, but that fairly measuring risk may not be feasible. For example, one sponsor said that it would be difficult to fairly measure and assess the risk factors used in setting risk-based premium rates and to make the results of these measurements transparent.

Finally, some sponsor advocates we spoke with questioned the need to increase premiums at all. These advocates believe if more appropriate interest rates were used, the deficit would disappear, and no increase in premiums would be warranted.[70]

MOVING TO A RISK - BASED PREMIUM STRUCTURE POSES VARIOUS CHALLENGES

The process of redesigning and implementing a more risk-based premium structure poses a number of operational challenges. Additional data and analysis would be needed on the selected risk factors, with regular monitoring to ensure that the data are accurate and up-to-date. PBGC is uniquely situated to take on this complex task, but if granted the statutory authority to do so, the agency could then face a number of additional administrative challenges concerning governance, transparency, and sponsor recourse.

Additional Data and Analysis Would Be Needed

The rate-setting entity responsible for implementation of a risk-based premium structure likely would require access to financial and other firm-specific information to provide a sound technical basis for the underlying parameters of a risk-based premium regime. The specific types of information needed would depend on the specific factors selected, but the information currently being collected may not be sufficient in some cases. For example, PBGC currently obtains information about plans from data reported by plan sponsors on the Form 5500 and under section 4010 of ERISA. Plan sponsors are required to submit the Form 5500 annually to Labor, Internal Revenue Service, and PBGC.[71] This form includes information about the level of plan underfunding (which is currently captured in the variable-rate premium) and the investment mix of plan assets (which is a potential risk factor that could be incorporated). The other main source of information, data reported under section 4010 of ERISA, is submitted to PBGC by plan sponsors only if certain criteria are met.[72] The PPA revised those criteria, and according to PBGC officials, some plans are no longer required to provide information under section 4010 of ERISA even though they still pose an increased risk to PBGC.[73]

PBGC also obtains information about the financial health of plan sponsors through its Early Warning Program, which is responsible for monitoring companies that are deemed to pose a greater risk to PBGC because they are financially troubled or have a significantly underfunded pension plan.[74] This program uses information from a variety of sources in conducting its work, including credit ratings, financial information services, news databases, and information from Labor, the Internal Revenue Service, and the Securities and Exchange Commission. While information gathered through the Early Warning Program would be relevant to the potential risk factor of a company's financial health, the program does not systematically gather data for all plan sponsors, and PBGC may be limited in its ability to use some credit rating data to assess risk within a redesigned premium structure.[75]

Other government agencies with risk-based premiums have established reliable sources of needed information to support their premium structures. For example, the FDIC relies entirely on pre-existing sources of information and technical resources to assess risk for its risk-based premiums. FDIC obtains information on institutions' aggregate assets from the quarterly reports submitted by each bank. FDIC's CAMELS ratings are developed during on-site examinations of each institution, during which regulators more closely assess institutions' exposure to risk. These quarterly reports and on-site examinations existed prior to FDIC's shift to risk-based premiums, so FDIC did not need to gather additional information or develop new expertise when it implemented its risk-based premium structure.

Alternatively, in the UK, PPF (the UK's pension insurance agency) relies on information obtained annually through an online exchange for the information needed to implement the risk-based premium structure.[76] PPF calculates its risk-based premiums based on three risk factors: level of underfunding, risk posed by the plan's investment strategy, and risk of sponsor insolvency (or bankruptcy). The exchange provides the agency with information on a plan's level of underfunding and how plan assets are allocated across investments with different levels of risk. According to a PPF May 2011 policy statement, beginning with plan year 2012/13, very large plan sponsors—those with plan liabilities of £1.5 billion or greater (about $2.35 billion in U.S. dollars)—are required to submit additional information about their investments, while submission is optional for smaller plans. To assess sponsors' risk of insolvency, PPF currently relies on Dun & Bradstreet's failure scores—a measure of the likelihood of sponsor bankruptcy—and applies its own schedule of premium rates for differing Dun & Bradstreet scores. These rates build in a risk margin equivalent to the charge an insurer would make for costs of capital held for unexpected claims.[77]

However, PBGC's lack of similar regulatory authority compared with FDIC and UK's PPF could limit wholesale applicability of these other entities' premium frameworks for PBGC. For example, according to PBGC officials, the agency has virtually no regulatory authority and no examination authority, and thus cannot routinely obtain the information that the FDIC has at its disposal as a regulator. Similarly, PPF functions as part of a larger pension regulatory structure, which includes The Pensions Regulator—the agency responsible for regulating pension plans in the UK. One of The Pensions Regulator's stated objectives is to reduce the risk that PPF will need to take on unfunded liabilities. On its website, The Pensions Regulator lists examples of the regulatory actions it can take against plan sponsors to protect the security of participants' benefits. In contrast, the oversight of pensions in the United States is more diffused with different authorities residing within the Employee Benefits Security Administration, the Internal Revenue Service, and PBGC. PBGC officials noted that the President's proposal for a more risk-based premium structure called for an analysis and public comment process, in part, to help address PBGC's limited authority regarding the additional data and analysis needed to implement such a structure.

Other differences between PBGC and the UK's PPF may also limit the applicability of PPF's premium framework for PBGC. For example, the governance structure of U.S. single-employer pensions and UK pensions differ significantly. According to The Pensions Regulator's website, UK pension law requires that at least one-third of individuals responsible for administering the plan, or plan trustees, must be selected by plan participants. In contrast, there is no requirement for stakeholder representation among fiduciaries of U.S. single-employer plans.[78]

Stronger Governance and Oversight Would Be Needed

Implementing a more risk-based premium structure creates governance challenges whether authority for premium setting rests with Congress, PBGC, or another entity. Premiums for PBGC's single-employer program—both the flat-rate premium and the variable-rate premium— are currently set by statute and PBGC lacks the statutory authority to modify premium rates and structures on its own.[79] Although legislation has been enacted to periodically adjust the level of premiums, this process has resulted in rates that do not adequately reflect the risk to PBGC's financial condition.

In moving to more risk-based premium structure, Congress could decide to enact new premium rates directly. For example, Congress could establish a formula under which both financial risk and underfunding would jointly determine a plan's premium (as shown earlier on table 6). The legislation could include fixed dollar caps (as in MAP-21) or limits on the annual percentage change in premiums.

But even if Congress were to decide to delegate authority over setting premium rates under a new structure, it could still maintain an important role in the process. For example, some experts we spoke with suggested that Congress could establish the broad framework for incorporating additional risk factors into PBGC's premium structure, while leaving the detailed mechanics of how to construct such a structure to others with greater technical expertise. In addition, a number of pension experts we spoke with said that congressional oversight would be useful during the premium redesign process. Many supported regular reporting by PBGC to Congress on progress in developing and implementing a risk-based premium structure, with some going further to suggest that PBGC report its proposed changes to the Congress with changes taking effect only if enacted into law.[80]

While Congress has the authority to set and change premiums, PBGC has considerable expertise in reviewing relevant data to assist with designing a more risk-based premium structure. In many ways, as the implementing agency of the current premium structure, PBGC is uniquely situated to obtain and analyze the complex data needed to design and implement a more risk-based premium structure. However, if PBGC were granted statutory authority to redesign its premium structure, stronger governance and oversight of the agency may be required. MAP-21, enacted in July 2012, included certain changes to strengthen PBGC's governance structure. For example, the act requires the Board of Directors to meet at least four times a year and convene one joint meeting per year with the PBGC Advisory Committee. It also requires the addition of a PBGC risk management officer, [81] a participant and plan sponsor advocate,[82] and a study of the governing structure of PBGC.[83] MAP-21 also requires the Board of Directors to establish a policy to identify and mitigate potential conflicts of interest.[84]

However, even with the recent legislative changes, concerns with PBGC's governance structure with respect to implementing a risk-based premium structure would persist. Our prior work has found that the current size of PBGC's board is not sufficient to include the diverse set of interests or expertise needed to provide policy direction for PBGC.[85] Some of the pension experts we spoke with maintained that PBGC's current board structure is adequate to provide sufficient oversight, while others echoed our concerns, commenting that the Board of Directors needs to be more active and reflect a wider range of technical expertise and stakeholder interests should it be granted additional statutory authority with respect to implementing a more risk-based premium structure.

At the same time, some experts we spoke with also noted that certain safeguards could be put in place to help mitigate such concerns. For example, special temporary commissions—such as an independent advisory committee comprised of a range of stakeholders and experts— are a tool that can be used to formulate recommendations for specific policy areas. [86] Along these lines, some pension experts we spoke with suggested establishing an independent advisory committee—comprised of knowledgeable representatives from a range of fields including academics, actuarial and labor experts—to play a formal role in the premium redesign process. Such an advisory committee could help ensure that the premium redesign process reflects stakeholder concerns and needed expertise.[87] A number of redesign suggestions from various stakeholder groups have already emerged, such as setting caps on premium increases, offering a transition period for new rates, using an independent third-party measure of creditworthiness, and reducing adverse effects on sponsors produced by economic downturns and higher premiums by smoothing (averaging) premium rates over several years to reduce volatility.

Greater Transparency and Provisions for Recourse Would Be Necessary

A more risk-based premium structure would likely spur demand for procedures to increase the transparency of PBGC's policies and technical work to bolster confidence in the agency's ability to effectively implement such a system, including procedures for recourse in the event of the assessment of excessive or inaccurate premiums. Various concerns have been raised about the agency's lack of transparency, especially related to the technical tools used to inform policy changes. Such a perceived lack of transparency could hamper public confidence in the agency's efforts to implement a redesigned premium structure.

More specifically, some pension experts and plan sponsors we spoke with expressed concerns that PBGC's operations are not clear or easily understandable, making it difficult to assess the accuracy and reasonableness of its estimates. Some pointed to the PIMS model, which is used to project the possible impact of policy changes on the agency's finances. Although PIMS has undergone several external reviews by academics and the Society of Actuaries, among others,[88] concerns about the model persist. In May 2012, such concerns were exacerbated by release of a PBGC Inspector General report critical of PIMS' internal controls.[89] The issues surrounding PIMS have contributed to a lack of confidence in the agency and its public estimates among some in the plan sponsor and business communities.[90]

To increase the transparency of any processes that PBGC may be authorized to use to calculate risk factors, experts we spoke with generally supported adopting various other safeguards,[91] including the following:

- *Disclosing the methodology for creating risk profiles.* Require publication of the methodology used to create sponsors' risk profiles, while continuing to safeguard any non-publicly available information used in actually calculating risk-based premiums. 92
- *Publishing a risk-based premium schedule.* Require publication of a schedule that includes information such as premium rates and key dates for plan sponsors.
- *Soliciting public feedback.* In redesigning the premium structure, include a mechanism for soliciting public feedback—either through a public comment period or by holding public hearings—to improve the transparency of the process.[93]
- *Increasing congressional reporting and oversight.* Require PBGC to regularly report to Congress—either through testimony or written report— on progress made on implementing a risk-based premium structure. Such reports could contain specific information related to risk-based premiums, such as risk measures, cross indicators, and premiums by industry.

Finally, it is also important to bolster confidence in a redesigned premium structure by including provisions for recourse if a sponsor wishes to appeal its risk assessment. For example, PPF officials told us that in the UK, they were required to implement an appeals process allowing plan sponsors to request a review of their case if they believed there was a mistake in the calculation of the plan-based premium or the underfunding component of the risk-based premium.[94] They also noted that in the initial year during which risk-based premiums were levied (2006/07), sponsors filed approximately 200 appeals (or approximately 3 percent of an estimated 7,800 plans).[95] However, 5 years later, in the most recent premium year (2011/12), the number of appeals had dropped to 70 (or approximately 1 percent of an estimated 6,550 plans),[96] suggesting that sponsor confidence in PPF has grown.

CONCLUSION

PBGC faces a number of challenges in its role as insurer and protector of pension benefits under DB systems that millions of Americans depend on for their retirement security. To remain financially solvent, PBGC relies on returns on its investments as well as premiums. However, the number of DB plans has been falling and premium rates have not adequately reflected the level of risk posed to PBGC for losses resulting from new claims. If PBGC's current financial challenges are not addressed, the agency could ultimately face insolvency, potentially resulting in a need for legislative changes either to make painful reductions to participant benefits or significant additional increases in premiums, or to provide for taxpayers to cover these costs. A key objective of redesigning PBGC's premium structure would be to ensure that premium revenue keeps pace with future claims and that the new structure is designed to decrease cross-subsidization between financially healthy and unhealthy sponsors. By adopting a structure that allows rates to better align with the risk posed by individual plans and sponsors, Congress has an opportunity to help PBGC contain its deficit and strengthen PBGC's ability to remain solvent into the future.

Determining whether—and if so, how—to redesign and implement a more risk-based premium structure will require new tools, new data, and new processes. PBGC's hypothetical model created to illustrate different premium options and its analyses of the effects of incorporating an additional risk factor are extremely useful tools for informing the debate on how PBGC's premium structure might be redesigned. However, these efforts are only a first step. As illustrated by other risk-based premium structures implemented in this country by the FDIC and abroad by the UK's pension insurance fund, options exist to establish risk-based premiums using a broad array of financial data. Much like these agencies' premium structures, PBGC premiums could be designed to identify each individual sponsor's unique risk profile and charge each sponsor a specific risk premium sufficient to cover that sponsor's risk. To ensure that any changes to PBGC's premium structure are designed and implemented in a reliable and fair way, decisions will need to be informed by a wide range of perspectives. The continuing involvement of stakeholders in the form of an advisory committee to assist with implementing these changes could be helpful in improving the transparency and legitimacy of the new system, whether Congress retains its premium-setting authority or determines that the authority for premium setting should rest with PBGC or another entity.

Moreover, should a more risk-based premium structure be adopted, it will be important for the responsible rate-setting entity to have access to the right information and expertise to adequately assess risk to incorporate any new risk factors into the process on an ongoing basis. Revising sponsors' financial reporting requirements—such as the reporting required under section 4010 of ERISA—could improve PBGC's ability to collect key information that may be necessary to help the agency estimate its risk exposure to future claims and strengthen implementation of any changes to the premium structure. It will also be important to ensure that the rate-setting entity has adequate expertise to conduct rational evaluations of the future risk posed by plan sponsors in order to provide a sound basis for setting premiums accordingly in alignment with that risk. To this end, Congress has taken an important step with MAP-21 by establishing quality control requirements for PBGC, including an annual peer review of PIMS. Ensuring that this annual peer review includes review of the inputs and assumptions used in PIMS projections and resulting outputs, specifically as they relate to projecting PBGC's future financial condition, would further enhance the transparency and credibility of any calculations used to support a more risk-based premium structure.

Also, should a more risk-based premium structure be adopted, it will be important to identify the financial impact that risk-based premiums would have on plan sponsors and on the future of the DB system. A more fully risk-based premium structure would presumably redistribute costs onto plan sponsors posing the greatest risk to PBGC—sponsors who may be financially weak. Congress and PBGC will need to consider the impact of this added burden on these plan sponsors, particularly during weak economic periods.

MATTERS FOR CONGRESSIONAL CONSIDERATION

To help strengthen the PBGC insurance program, Congress should consider the following action:

1. Authorize redesign of PBGC's premium structure to more fully reflect the risk posed by plans and sponsors to the agency, such as by providing for the incorporation of additional risk factors.

In addition, to improve PBGC's ability to collect key information that may be necessary to help the agency estimate its risk exposure to future claims and strengthen implementation of any changes to the premium structure, Congress should consider the following action:

2. Provide PBGC with access to additional information needed to assess risk and assist in setting premiums, such as by expanding the criteria requiring plan sponsors to report under section 4010 of ERISA.

Moreover, to better understand the mechanics of how best to incorporate additional risk factors, improve transparency, and help inform the evaluation of the various redesign options, Congress should consider the following action:

3. Establish an independent premiums advisory committee reflecting a range of perspectives—including, for example, representatives from federal agencies, sponsors, actuaries, private insurers, and labor groups—to assist with such activities as developing the mechanics for incorporating additional risk factors and implementing new rates, as well as delineating a variety of alternative methods to address PBGC's deficit.

RECOMMENDATION FOR EXECUTIVE ACTION

To enhance understanding and better inform debate on the possible effects of moving to a more risk-based premium structure, during consideration of various redesign options and after a redesign may be authorized, we recommend that the Director of PBGC take the following action:

1. Continue to develop PBGC's hypothetical model, analyzing various premium redesign options and their impacts on sponsors, and report the results to Congress. As part of these analyses, PBGC should evaluate the potential effects on sponsors of incorporating additional risk factors, such as company financial health and plan investment mix, and include an assessment to identify any potentially disproportional hardships on smaller companies that may result from the redistribution of higher rates to riskier sponsors.

AGENCY COMMENTS AND OUR EVALUATION

We obtained written comments on a draft of this report from PBGC. PBGC generally agreed with our findings and conclusions. PBGC believes that basing premiums on the actual risk of plan terminations would encourage and reward companies to keep DB plans, and that under a more risk-based approach, many financially sound companies would see their premiums decrease. PBGC also agrees with our finding that moving to more risk-based premiums is not likely to drive sponsors to abandon their DB plans, but characterized our analysis as showing that such claims have no evidence to support them. We would like to clarify that, in our previous work, we found that sponsors mentioned factors other than excessive premiums as the primary reasons for freezing or terminating their DB plans. We did not intend to imply that such concerns about the potential effects of risk-based premiums were unfounded or without any supporting evidence.

PBGC agrees with our finding that there are important implementation concerns in moving to a more risk-based premium structure and characterized our suggested ways to address these concerns as constructive, warranting further discussion. For example, some of these concerns could be addressed by Congress simply establishing a more comprehensive risk-based approach statutorily rather than delegating premium-setting authority to another entity such as PBGC.

PBGC supports our recommendation for agency action—specifically, that PBGC should conduct further analyses of premium options. PBGC notes that it is committed to continued development of the databases, models, and analyses of various premium redesign options and their impacts on sponsors, and to report the results of these analyses to Congress. We welcome this commitment, as we believe that such efforts can contribute to adoption of a more effective and equitable rate-setting system, especially if these efforts include an evaluation of the potential for any disproportional hardships on smaller companies that may result from a more comprehensive risk-based structure. PBGC supported our matters for congressional consideration in its letter and technical comments, with respect to authorizing a more risk-based premium structure, providing PBGC with improved access to key information concerning plan sponsors' financial health, and establishing an independent premiums advisory committee reflecting a range of perspectives to improve transparency in the premium redesign process.

The Department of the Treasury also provided technical comments, which are incorporated into the report where appropriate. In addition, we received technical comments on certain segments of the draft report from PPF and FDIC, and have incorporated their comments where appropriate, as well.

Sincerely yours,
Charles A. Jeszeck
Director, Education, Workforce, and Income Security Issues

APPENDIX I: RECENT LEGISLATION RELATED TO THE PENSION BENEFIT GUARANTY CORPORATION

On July 6, 2012, the President signed into law the Moving Ahead for Progress in the 21st Century Act (MAP-21).[1] Although pensions were not the primary purpose of the act, it included several provisions that pertain to the Pension Benefit Guaranty Corporation (PBGC). For example, the act changed the process for determining defined benefit (DB) plan funding requirements, increased premium rates for sponsors of single-employer and multiemployer DB plans insured by PBGC, and included several provisions to improve the governance of PBGC. Sections of the act related to PBGC are briefly summarized below, along with a table detailing the preliminary revenue scoring by the Joint Committee on Taxation for these changes.

Part I—Pension Funding Stabilization

Sec. 40211. Pension Funding Stabilization

The act changed how the minimum funding required for a single-employer plan may be determined.

Specifically, it provided for adjustment of interest rates to be used in determining a plan's funding target. Plans that take advantage of this provision in determining their required minimum funding must provide information on the impact of electing to do so in their annual funding notices.

PART II—PBGC Premiums

Sec. 40221. Single-employer plan annual premium rates.

Sec. 40222. Multiemployer annual premium rates.

The act increases PBGC premium rates for both single-employer and multiemployer DB plans.

Effective beginning in 2013, the act changes the flat and variable premium rates and puts a cap on the variable-rate premium. Each flat or variable rate is subject to a different inflation adjustment, and the variable-rate premium cap has its own inflation adjustment.

PART III—Improvements of PBGC

Sec. 40231. Pension Benefit Guaranty Corporation Governance Improvement.

The act amended the Employee Retirement Income Security Act of 1974 (ERISA) provisions relating to the PBGC Board of Directors, Advisory Committee, Director and other PBGC officials in various ways. Among other things, with respect to the Board of Directors, it established that a majority of its members constitutes a quorum and the vote of a majority of board members present shall be an act of the board.

Under the provision, the board is to meet no less than four times a year with not fewer than two members present. At least one of those meetings must be with the PBGC Advisory Committee. It also provided that the PBGC Inspector General is to report to the board and at least twice a year attend a board meeting to report on PBGC operations. Furthermore, the provision clarifies the role of the General Counsel, and expressly provides that the Inspector General and the Inspector General legal counsel are independent of PBGC management and its General Counsel. The act includes specific requirements to PBGC's Board of Directors and Director to avoid conflicts of interest and provides for PBGC to have a risk management officer. It expressly provided that the PBGC Board of Directors is ultimately responsible for overseeing PBGC and that the Director is directly accountable to the Board of Directors and can be removed by the Board of Directors or the President. It also set the Director's term at 5 years unless removed before the expiration of the term by the President or the Board of Directors.

The act also stated the sense of Congress that (1) the Board of Directors should form committees, including an Audit Committee and an Investment Committee composed of at least two members, to enhance the overall effectiveness of the board, and (2) the Advisory Committee should provide the board with policy recommendations regarding changes to law that would be beneficial to PBGC or the voluntary private pension system.

The act also directs PBGC, not later than 90 days after enactment, to contract with the National Academy of Public Administration to conduct a study to include (1) a review of governance structures of organizations analogous to PBGC and (2) recommendations with respect to various topics relating to the Board of Directors, such as composition, procedures, and policies to enhance congressional oversight.

The results of the study are to be reported within a year of initiation of the study to the to the Committee on Health, Education, Labor, and Pensions and the Committee on Finance in the Senate; and the Committee on Education and the Workforce and the Committee on Ways and Means in the House of Representatives.

Sec. 40232. Participant and plan sponsor advocate.

The act requires the Board of Directors to choose a Participant and Plan Sponsor Advocate from the candidates nominated by the PBGC Advisory Committee.

Among other things, this advocate is to act as a liaison between PBGC and participants in terminated pension plans, ensure that participants receive everything they are entitled to under law, and provide plan sponsors with assistance in resolving disputes with PBGC.

Each year, the advocate will provide a report on these activities to the Committee on Health, Education, Labor, and Pensions and the Committee on Finance in the Senate; and the Committee on Education and the Workforce and the Committee on Ways and Means in the House of Representatives.

The report is to summarize the issues raised by participants and plan sponsors, making recommendations for changes to improve the system.

Table 9. Preliminary Joint Committee on Taxation Score of Revenue Changes Caused by Surface Transportation Conference Report Related to Pension Funding Stabilization and PBGC Premium Provisions, Fiscal Years 2012-2022

Category	2012	2013	2014	2015	2016	2017	2018	2019	2020	2021	2022	2012-2017	2012-2022
Pension funding stabilization	595	2391	4576	5144	3765	1671	274	-807	-2328	-3121	-2766	18142	9394
Cap single-employer variable rate	0	0	-140	-260	-280	-130	-60	-20	-10	-10	-10	-810	-920
Increased flat-rate premiums	0	200	400	400	500	530	570	600	630	630	670	2030	5130
Variable-rate premiums	0	0	0	760	1190	810	570	370	290	330	330	2760	4710
Multiemployer programs	0	20	15	15	25	25	25	30	30	30	40	100	255
Interaction	0	0	0	50	227	231	256	208	209	159	110	508	1450
Extension for Transfers/420 for life insurance	0	0	20	41	42	43	44	45	47	18	24	145	354
Net total revenue increases	595	2611	4871	6150	5469	3180	1679	426	-1132	-1964	-1602	22875	20373

Source: Joint Committee on Taxation.

Sec. 40233. Quality control procedures for the Pension Benefit Guaranty Corporation.

The act requires PBGC to contract with a capable agency or organization independent from PBGC, such as the Social Security Administration, to conduct an annual peer review of PBGC's Single-Employer and Multiemployer Pension Insurance Modeling Systems (PIMS). The first reviews must be initiated no later than 3 months after enactment of the act.

The act also requires PBGC to develop written quality review policies and procedures for all modeling and actuarial work performed by PBGC's Policy, Research, and Analysis Department, and conduct a record management and record keeping review.

Finally, it requires PBGC to provide a timetable for addressing outstanding recommendations made by the Inspector General relating to the Policy, Research, and Analysis Department and the Benefits Administration and Payment Department.

Sec. 40234. Line of credit repeal.

The act repeals section 4005(c) of ERISA,[2] which permitted PBGC to issue notes or other obligations in an amount up to $100,000,000.

APPENDIX II: PRESIDENT'S FISCAL YEAR 2013 BUDGET PROPOSAL FOR PBGC

The Budget of the United States Government, Fiscal Year 2013, includes information on the President's budget priorities organized by agency. Administratively, PBGC is an entity within of the Department of Labor. In the President's budget, one of the funding highlights for the Department of Labor includes the following: "Safeguards workers' pensions by encouraging companies to fully fund their employees' promised pension benefits and assuring the long-term solvency of the Federal pension insurance system." The President proposes accomplishing this by (1) raising $16 billion in additional premium revenue over 10 years through phased-in increases to PBGC's flat- and variable-rate premiums, and (2) giving the PBGC's Board of Directors the authority to adjust premiums.[1]

Table 10. Proposed Budget Savings Listed under PBGC

Deficit increases (+) or decreases (–) in millions of dollars												
											Totals	
	2013	**2014**	**2015**	**2016**	**2017**	**2018**	**2019**	**2020**	**2021**	**2022**	**2013-2017**	**2013-2022**
Improve PBGC solvency	—	-81	-1,828	-2,275	-2,316	-2,067	-1,713	-1,616	-1,874	-2,210	-6,500	-15,980

Source: Budget proposal, p. 231, Table S–9. Mandatory and Receipt Proposals (excerpt under Labor).

Excerpts from the President's Budget Proposal

(1) The administration proposed raising $16 billion in additional premium revenue over 10 years by raising $4 billion in additional flat-rate premiums and $12 billion in additional variable-rate premiums (see table 10). Relevant excerpts from the budget proposal are provided below.

- **Strengthen the Safety Net for Workers' Retirement Benefits.** All Americans deserve a secure retirement. . . . The Pension Benefit Guaranty Corporation (PBGC), which protects the retirement security of 44 million workers in defined benefit pension plans, is also critical to the success of a robust pension system. When underfunded plans terminate, PBGC assumes responsibility for paying the insured benefits. PBGC is responsible for paying current and future retirement benefits to more than 1.5 million workers and retirees. PBGC receives no taxpayer financing and relies primarily on premiums paid by insured plans. PBGC premiums are currently much lower than what a private financial institution would charge for insuring the same risk and are insufficient for PBGC to meet its long-term obligations. As of the end of September 2011, PBGC faced a $26 billion deficit. The Administration proposes to encourage companies to fully fund their pension benefits and ensure PBGC's continued financial soundness by giving the PBGC Board the authority to adjust premiums to better account for the risk the agency is insuring. This proposal consists of two parts: a gradual increase in the single-employer flat-rate premium that will raise approximately $4 billion by 2022; and PBGC Board discretion to increase the single-employer variable-rate premium to raise $12 billion by 2022. This proposal would save $16 billion over the next decade. (p. 146)

(2) The President's fiscal year 2013 budget proposes giving the PBGC Board of Directors the authority to adjust premiums. Relevant excerpts from the budget proposal are provided below.

- **Shores Up the Pension Benefit Guaranty Corporation to Protect Worker Pensions.** The Pension Benefit Guaranty Corporation (PBGC) acts as a backstop to protect pension payments for workers whose companies have failed. Currently, the PBGC's pension insurance system is itself underfunded, and the PBGC's liabilities exceed its assets. The PBGC receives no taxpayer funds and its premiums are currently much lower than what a private financial institution would charge for insuring the same risk. The Budget proposes to give the PBGC Board the authority to adjust premiums and directs PBGC to take into account the risks that different sponsors pose to their retirees and to PBGC. This will both encourage companies to fully fund their pension benefits and ensure the continued financial soundness of PBGC. In order to ensure that these reforms are undertaken responsibly during challenging economic times, the Budget would require a year of study and public comment before any implementation and the gradual phasing-in of any premium increases. This proposal is estimated to save $16 billion over the next decade. (p. 147)

Rate Increases under the President's Proposal

PBGC estimated the increases in the flat and variable rates that would be needed to reach the administration's revenue targets over the 10-year period. PBGC estimated that the flat rate would need to double from the current rate of $35 per participant to $71 in 2022, and the variable rate would increase almost eight-fold from its current rate of $9 per $1,000 of underfunding to $71 in 2022 (see table 11).

Table 11. Increase in Premium Rates for the Single-Employer Program Estimated by PBGC for the President's Fiscal Year 2013 Budget, Fiscal Years 2013-2022

Premium rates	2013	2014	2015	2016	2017	2018	2019	2020	2021	2022
Flat rate (dollars charged per participant)[a]	$36.00	40.00	44.00	48.00	52.00	56.00	60.00	63.00	67.00	71.00
Variable rate (dollars charged per $1,000 of underfunding)[b]	$9.00	15.88	22.76	29.64	36.53	43.41	50.29	57.17	64.05	70.93

Source: GAO analysis of PBGC data.

[a]The flat-rate premium is calculated on a per participant basis. Under current law, the flat rate for fiscal year 2012 is $35 per participant, and is indexed to increases in the national average wage index, as determined by the Social Security Administration. 29 U.S.C. § 1306(a)(3)(A) and (F).

[b]The variable-rate premium is calculated based a plan's level of underfunding whereby every $1,000 of underfunding is multiplied by the rate. Under current law, the variable rate is $9 per every $1,000 of plan underfunding. 29 U.S.C. § 1306(a)(3)(F).

This estimate is based on PBGC's projections that assume plan participant levels would remain unchanged [2] and unfunded vested benefit levels would decline significantly over the next decade,[3] and that do not incorporate any additional risk factors into the variable rate. PBGC projected this decrease in underfunding (increase in funding) due to several factors,[4] including PPA funding requirements that will tend to bolster plan funding over this period.[5]

However, PBGC used PIMS to make assumptions about future unfunded vested benefit levels for estimating premium rates for the President's proposal, and PBGC officials recognize that uncertainty exists in the many economic factors and underlying assumptions used for this projection. In addition, the agency's Inspector General recently identified internal control deficiencies related to actuarial estimates used in the agency's PIMS model.[6] We reviewed the PIMS data provided to us and conducted a meeting with PBGC officials to discuss the reliability of these data and some of the data used in its 2010 exposure report. We determined that the PIMS data provided to us and used by PBGC in its report were sufficiently reliable to provide information on the approximate magnitude of PBGC's future financial condition and the mechanics of premium options.

Using the same assumptions PBGC used to estimate rates for the President's fiscal year 2013 budget, we estimated the increases in rates that would be needed to reach a revenue target of $23 billion, the current level of PBGC's deficit in the single-employer program. This scenario illustrates the increases in rates that would be required if no other sources of revenue were available to help address PBGC's deficit, such as returns on investment. We found that under this scenario, the flat-rate premium would need to increase to $75 and the variable-rate premium to $106 by fiscal year 2022.

APPENDIX III: FURTHER GAO ANALYSES OF A RISK-BASED PREMIUM OPTION

To better understand the impact on rates under one hypothetical risk-based option, we conducted additional analyses using data provided to us by PBGC from a premium option model PBGC designed to illustrate different premium scenarios. PBGC's model used 2010 data from a sample of 2,699 DB plans covering 27.5 million participants. The model covered 81 percent of all PBGC insured participants (33.8 million) in 2010.

First, we analyzed the sample data to determine how the plans would be distributed based on their financial health and funded status. Results are summarized in table 12.

Table 12. Distribution of Plans by Financial Health and Funded Status under a Hypothetical Risk-Based Option

		Funded status			
Financial health	**≥120%**	**≥90% to under 120%**	**75% to under 90%**	**<75%**	**Total plans**
Extremely healthy (1)	21	110	59	6	196
Very healthy (2)	58	349	155	24	586
Healthy (3)	55	527	367	68	1017
Risky (4)	20	215	203	85	523
Very risky (5)	15	118	178	66	377
Total	**169**	**1319**	**962**	**249**	**2699**

Source: GAO analysis of PBGC data from a sample of 2,699 defined benefit plans used in PBGC's hypothetical premium model.

Next, we analyzed the effect of the rate changes under this option on the sample based on the number of participants in the sample of plans used in PBGC's model, as shown in table 13. In total, we estimate that rates would decrease under the risk-based option over 2015 rates for plans covering a majority of participants in the sample when considering the per participant costs for sponsors, regardless of the funding status of a participant's plan or the financial health of the participant's sponsor.

We further analyzed the effect of the rate changes under this option on plans in PBGC's sample. As table 14 shows, the distributional effect of premium changes for plans using this option varies based on a sponsor's financial health and plan funding levels. We estimate that premiums for a majority of plans categorized as more financially healthy would decrease, due in part to the proposed increase in the flat rate to $49 per participant under the act compared to $44 per participant under this option. In the model, PBGC assumed that plans with 90 percent or greater funding levels and rated as either extremely healthy or very healthy for financial health would be considered as low risk for plan termination and would therefore not have a variable rate included in their premium calculation. We estimated that two-thirds of plans considered financially healthy would have their rates decreased and that nearly all plans considered less financially healthy would experience a rate increase under this option.

Table 13. Number and Percentage of Participants with Premium Rate Changes under One Hypothetical Risk-Based Option

	Premium rate change over 2015 per participant rate	
Plan funded status	**Number of participants in plans with increased rates (percent)**	**Number of participants in plans with decreased rates (percent)**
≥120%	904,921	1,238,648
	(42%)	(58%)
≥90% to under	7,158,249	9,948,743
120%	(42)	(58)
75% to under 90%	2,355,025	4,033,812
	(37)	(63)
<75%	1,375,433	491,817
	(74)	(26)
Plan financial health		
Extremely healthy	5,160	2,684,969
(1)	(less than 1%)	(100%)
Very healthy (2)	67,446	9,340,587
	(1)	(99)
Healthy (3)	4,858,897	3,083,163
	(61)	(39)
Risky (4)	3,603,325	390,053
	(90)	(10)
Very risky (5)	3,258,800	214,248
	(94)	(6)
More financially	4,931,503	15,108,719
healthy (1-3)	(25)	(75)
Less financially	6,862,125	604,301
healthy (4-5)	(92)	(8)

Source: GAO analysis of PBGC data from a sample of 2,699 defined benefit plans used in PBGC's hypothetical premium model.

Table 14. Number and Percentage of Plans with Premium Rate Changes under One Hypothetical Risk-Based Option

	Premium rate change over 2015 per participant rate	
Plan funded status	Number of plans with increased rates (percent)	Number of plans withdecreased rates (percent)
>120%	90 (53%)	79(47%)
>90% to under 120%	770 (58)	549(42)
75% to under 90%	408 (42)	554(58)
<75%	169 (68)	80(32)
Extremely healthy (1)	2 (1%)	194(99%)
Very healthy (2)	16 (3)	570(97)
Healthy (3)	598 (59)	419(41)

Table 14. (Continued)

	Premium rate change over 2015 per participant rate	
Plan funded status	Number of plans with increased rates (percent)	Number of plans withdecreased rates (percent)
Risky (4)	478 (91)	45(9)
Very risky (5)	343 (91)	34(9)
More financially healthy (1-3)	616 (34)	1183(66)
Less financially healthy (4-5)	821 (91)	79(9)

Source: GAO analysis of PBGC data from a sample of 2,699 defined benefit plans used in PBGC's hypothetical premium model.

APPENDIX IV: THE UNITED KINGDOM'S PENSION PROTECTION FUND'S PREMIUM STRUCTURE

The United Kingdom's (UK) Pension Protection Fund (PPF) employs a premium structure—which it refers to as a levy[1]— that includes a risk-based premium to help mitigate risk presented by sponsors of defined benefit (DB) plans.[2] Beginning with its second plan year in 2006/07, risk factors have been incorporated into premium rates. PPF has experienced a surplus in its net financial position when comparing its assets and its liabilities. As of March 31, 2011, PPF had a $1.08 billion surplus, an increase of $480 million over the previous year.

Features of PPF's Premium Structure

PPF sets a premium revenue target based on a long-term funding strategy of accumulating assets that are 10 percent larger than its liabilities. To meet its revenue target, PPF collects two types of premiums from plan sponsors: a risk-based premium and a plan-based premium. The risk-based premium is based on three risk factors-—a plan's asset investment mix, a plan's funding level, and risk of sponsor bankruptcy, which PPF refers to as insolvency risk. The plan-based premium is based on the size of a plan and its liabilities. For plan year 2012/13, PPF is using the following formula to calculate the plan-based and risk-based premiums:

Risk-based premium
underfunding risk modified by investment risk stress (U*Inv) x insolvency risk (P) x levy scaling factor (C)

Plan-based premium
.000085 (h) x smoothed liabilities (L)

Table 15 describes the different components of PPF's premium formula for plan year 2012/13.

Table 15. Components of the United Kingdom's Pension Protection Fund's Premium Formula, Plan Year 2012/13

Risk-based premium components	Description
Underfunding risk (U)	Represents the potential size of a plan's claim on PPF. Uis the underfunding amount of the plan determined by using the plan's assets and liabilities, taking account of any valid contingent asset arrangements and deficit-reduction contributions. Contingent assets are assets that a sponsor puts forth to reduce potential losses to PPF.[a] Asset and liability values used in calculating underfunding riskare adjusted based on an investment risk methodology (see below.)
Investment risk (INV)	An adjustment made to underfunding risk that takes into account risk posed by a sponsor's investmentstrategy for its plans' assets. Different asset classes used for investing—such as bonds, equities, commodities, and hedge funds—are stressed according to risk and the value of assets in each asset class is increased or decreased as appropriate by the corresponding asset stress percentage INV.
Insolvency risk (P)	Represents the likelihood of a plan's sponsor becoming insolvent and the plan potentially becoming a claim on PPF. Pis a measure of risk of insolvency of the sponsor, taking into account the plan structure. Measures of risk insolvency are provided to PPF by Dun & Bradstreet. Pmay be modified where there is a Type A contingent asset, which is a parent or group company guaranty to cover PPF losses should the plan terminate. PPF uses Dun & Bradstreet failure scores to estimate a sponsor's insolvency risk. Based on this score, a sponsor is placed in one of 10 premium bands, with each band assigned an associated premium rate. The premium rate for each band combines a component based on the Dun & Bradstreet probabilities of insolvency for the failure scores in that band plus a risk margin based on unexpected risk for that band.
Premium scaling factor (C)	Scales down risk-based premium so that together with the plan-based levies, PPF will ensure that the total premium collected matches the premium estimate, which is based on long-term risk exposure. In the premium formula, this is represented as Cand is .89 for 2012/13.

Table 15. (Continued)

Risk-based premium components	Description
Plan-based premium components	
Multiplier (H)	H is a plan-based premium multiplier applied to every plan to cover the costs of capping[b] the highest risk-based premiums—about 10% of the premium.
Liabilities (L)	L is the plan's estimated liabilities as of a certain date.

Source: GAO analysis of PPF data.

[a]PPF describes contingent assets as those assets that occur when another company under the same corporate umbrella as a plan sponsor guaranties a portion of the plan's liabilities, thereby reducing the plan sponsor's risk of entering bankruptcy. Continent assets can also occur when a plan sponsor (or a company under the same corporate umbrella) pledges assets—a bank account, land, or securities—that will go to the pension plans if a sponsor enters bankruptcy or when a party outside the sponsor's corporate umbrella guaranties a portion of the plan's liabilities, either through a letter of credit or a bank guaranty.

[b]The risk-based premium is also capped to protect the most vulnerable plans. The cap for 2012/13 is 75 basis points (0.75 percent) of smoothed liabilities. Where the risk-based premium calculated using the above formula exceeds 0.75 percent of a plan's liabilities, the cap is applied and the premium is decreased accordingly.

PPF allows plan sponsors to lower their premium by pledging contingent assets, which can be used to cover potential losses from underfunded plans that terminate and reduce the risk posed to PPF, and thus reduce their risk-based premium. PPF defines contingent assets in a number of ways. Type A contingent assets occur when another company under the same corporate umbrella as a plan sponsor guaranties a portion of the plan's liabilities, thereby reducing the plan sponsor's risk of entering bankruptcy. Type B continent assets occur when a plan sponsor (or a company under the same corporate umbrella) pledges assets—a bank account, land, or securities—that will go to the pension plans if a sponsor enters bankruptcy. Type C contingent assets occur when a party outside the sponsor's corporate umbrella guaranties a portion of the plan's liabilities, either through a letter of credit or a bank guaranty.

Both Type B and C contingent assets lower the liabilities that PPF would take over in the event that the sponsor was to enter bankruptcy and transfer its plan(s) to the agency.

PPF's Funding Strategy

PPF's funding strategy is formulated to meet the agency's stated longterm goal of accumulating assets that are 10 percent larger than the agency's liabilities by 2030, which represents a state of self-sufficiency.[3] Initially, the premium estimate (the amount PPF aims to collect) reflected a "top down" approach in which PPF would decide upon the total level of premiums that it deemed appropriate in a given year, and adjusted the premium parameters accordingly on an annual basis. Beginning with the 2012/13 plan year, the funding strategy is revised to reflect a "bottom up" approach in which the parameters will be fixed for 3 years and, ideally, remain stable for 3 years between reviews, with the amount collected, floating with changes in risk.

Potential Applicability of PPF's Premium Structure for PBGC

Specific components of PPF's premium structure—such as use of additional risk factors for sponsor financial health and plan investment strategy, setting rates based on long-term budget estimates, and smoothing techniques—might have applicability for PBGC.[4] However, there are substantial regulatory and fiduciary differences between PPF and PBGC. For example, PPF functions as part of a larger pension regulatory structure, which includes The Pension Regulator. One of The Pensions Regulator's stated objectives is to reduce the risk that PPF will need to take on unfunded liabilities, and the agency has statutory authority to work with plan sponsors to mitigate these risks through increasing plan funding levels and other measures. In addition, UK pension law requires that at least one-third of individuals responsible for administering the plan, or plan trustees, must be selected by plan participants, while there is no requirement for stakeholder representation among fiduciaries of U.S. plans.

APPENDIX V: OVERVIEW OF PENSION BENEFIT GUARANTY CORPORATION'S PROCESS FOR CALCULATING ITS DEFICIT

As required under ERISA,[1] each year, PBGC calculates the corporation's net financial position by determining the values of its assets, offset by the value of its liabilities, for the single-employer and multiemployer programs combined. According to PBGC, a primary objective of its financial statements, and specifically its net financial position, is to provide information that is useful in assessing the agency's present and future ability to ensure that its plan beneficiaries receive benefits when due. Although long-term projections inherently contain a significant degree of uncertainty, a surplus net financial position signifies that, based on the assumptions used, PBGC estimates that it has sufficient assets to pay all current and future guarantied benefit obligations; a deficit net financial position signifies that its assets are not sufficient to pay all future obligations. The deficit is calculated in conformance with generally accepted accounting principles, which, among other things, require making estimates and assumptions that affect the reported amounts of liabilities as of the date of the statement and that may change over time. In particular, liabilities included in the single-employer deficit calculation include those from claims already incurred and claims deemed probable in the near term, but not future claims beyond that.[2] The main components of PBGC's assets and liabilities and descriptions of how PBGC determines the values for each of those components are summarized in table 16. The amounts of assets and liabilities in these various categories, for fiscal year-end 2011, can be found in table 17 later in this section.

Table 16. Main Components of Assets and Liabilities Included in PBGC's Statements of Financial Condition

Asset components	Description of valuation
Investments, at market	Investment assets are valued based on market prices, specifically, on the last sale of a listed security, on the mean of the "bid-and-ask" for nonlisted securities, or on a valuation model in the case of fixed income securities that are not actively traded.[a] These valuations are determined as of the end of each fiscal year. Purchases and sales of securities are recorded on the trade date. PBGCmarks a plan's assets to market and any increase or decrease in the market value of a plan's assetsoccurring after the date on which the plan is terminated must, by law, be credited to or suffered by PBGC.
Receivables, net (including premiums and investment income)[b]	Premiums receivable represent the estimated earned but unpaid portion of premiums and past due premiums deemed collectible, including penalties and interest. Investment income is accrued as earned.
Cash and cash equivalents	Cash includes cash on hand and demand deposits. Cash equivalents are investments with original maturities of 1 business day and highly liquid investments that are readily convertible into cash within 1 business day.

Asset components	Description of valuation
Securities lending collateral	PBGC's custodian bank requires collateral that equals 102% to 105% of the securities lent. The custodian bank either receives cash or noncash as collateral or returns collateral to cover mark-to-market changes.
Capitalized assets, net	Capitalized assets include furniture and fixtures, electronic processing equipment and internal-use software. These costs are shown net of accumulated depreciation and amortization.
Liability components	
Total present value of future benefits, net	Net liabilities for future pension benefits that PBGC is or will be obligated to pay the participants of single-employer plans terminated and trusteed, in accordance with the limits specified in ERISA, and plans that have $50 million or more of underfunding that PBGC believes will probably terminate in the near future.[c]
Total present value of nonrecoverable future financial assistance	The estimated value of nonrecoverable future financial assistance to multiemployer plans that are not able to meet their benefit obligations.[d] including probable insolvent plans.
Payables, net (including unearned premiums, amounts due for purchases of securities and derivative contracts)[b]	The liability for unearned premiums represents an estimate of payments received during the fiscal year that cover the portion of a plan's year after PBGC's fiscal year-end. Securities sold under repurchase agreements are valued at the amounts at which the securities well be subsequently reacquired.
Net position (loss)	Total assets minus total liabilities.

Source: PBGC's 2011 Annual Report.

[a] An investment valuation model is a widely accepted method used in finance to compute the current value of an asset based on statistical inputs for cash flow expectations.

[b] In addition, derivative financial instruments are recorded at fair value and are included on the Statements of Financial Condition as investments and derivative contracts. Swaps are netted rather than recorded at gross levels for the individual contracts as "Receivables, net – Derivative contracts" and "Derivative contracts" (liabilities). PBGC invests in and discloses its derivative investments in accordance with the guidance contained in the FASB Accounting Standards Codification Section 815, Derivatives and Hedging.

[c] PBGC may classify an underfunded plan as a probable termination when, among other things, the plan's sponsor is in liquidation under federal or state bankruptcy laws.

[d] In accordance with Title IV of ERISA, PBGC provides financial assistance to multiemployer plans, in the form of loans, to enable the plans to pay guarantied benefits to participants and reasonable administrative expenses. 29 U.S.C. § 1431. These loans, issued in exchange for interest-bearing promissory notes, constitute an obligation of each plan.

PBGC's Assumptions in Valuing Future Benefit Payments

Changes to the underlying assumptions used to value liabilities can have a material effect on PBGC's net financial position and on any conclusions drawn about PBGC's ability to pay all current and future guarantied benefit obligations (from claims already incurred and those deemed probable in the near term) from assets on hand. According to PBGC, liabilities under the single-employer program are valued by estimating the present value of future benefits expected to be paid—that is, PBGC uses certain assumptions to adjust the value of future benefit payments to reflect the time value of money (by discounting) and the probability of payment (by means of decrements, such as for death or retirement). According to agency officials, the method the agency uses to account for liabilities is similar to the "mark to market" practices being required of private sector sponsors of single-employer DB plans, in accordance with FASB.[3] The calculation requires an assumption about interest rates, which reflects how much could be earned in the future from investing today's dollars. Assuming a lower interest rate increases the present value of future payments or benefits.[4]

PBGC develops its assumptions on discount rates based on group annuity prices,[5] identified through a group annuity survey conducted by the American Council of Life Insurers. PBGC maintains that the annuity prices found on the survey reflect rates at which its liabilities (net of administrative expenses) could be settled in the market at September 30 for the respective year via single-premium nonparticipating group annuities issued by private insurers.[6]

PBGC notes that many factors, including Federal Reserve policy, changing expectations about longevity risk, and competitive market conditions may affect these survey rates. Using data from the annuity survey, PBGC establishes two interest rate factors to compute estimates of the present value of its liabilities—the "select" and "ultimate" rates.[7] A decline in PBGC's asset values can be particularly problematic if these interest rates remain low or fall, which raises PBGC's liabilities, all else equal.

PBGC also notes that, over time, actuarial adjustments may occur as the result of new data (e.g., mortality experience, revised participant data), as well as from changes in valuation methodology, such as estimating liabilities on a group basis ("nonseriatum") versus calculating a separate liability for each person ("seriatum"). Liabilities also will grow with the passage of time (as future benefit payments draw closer to payment), will decrease as benefits are paid out (discharging part of the liability), and will change with changes in interest rates and changes in other actuarial assumptions. These adjustments represent the change in the present value of future benefits that results from applying actuarial assumptions in the calculation of liabilities.[8]

PBGC's Fiscal Year 2011 Financial Statement

For fiscal year-end 2011, PBGC reported net accumulated deficit of approximately $26.04 billion. To estimate the present value of future benefits, PBGC used a 20-year select interest factor of 4.31 percent followed by an ultimate factor of 4.26 percent for the remaining years. PBGC strengthened its mortality assumptions in 2011 (that is, it assumed longer life expectancy), which resulted in higher interest factors than would have been estimated under the previous mortality assumption.[9] In addition, PBGC has estimated that as of September 30, 2011, 135 multiemployer plans[10] will exhaust plan assets and need financial assistance from PBGC to pay guarantied benefits and plan administrative expenses.[11] A summary of PBGC's deficit calculation for fiscal year-end 2011 is found in table 17.

Table 17. PBGC Statements of Financial Condition for its Single-Employer and Multiemployer Programs, Fiscal Year 2011

Dollars in millions			
	Single-employer program	**Multiemployer program**	**Single- employer and multiemployer combined**
Assets:			
Investments, at market	$66,271	$1,720	$67,991
Receivables, net (including premiums)	3,049	13	3,062
Cash and cash equivalents	5,021	5	5,026
Securities lending collateral	4,587	0	4,587
Capitalized assets, net	32	1	33
Total assets	**78,960**	**1,739**	**80,699**
Liabilities:			
Total present value of future benefits, net	92,953	1	92,954
Total present value of nonrecoverable future financial assistance	0	4,475	4,475
Total payables	9,273	33	9,306
Total liabilities	**102,226**	**4,509**	**106,735**
Net position (loss)	**(23,266)**	**(2,770)**	**(26,036)**

Source: PBGC's 2011 Annual Report.

PBGC's Historical Net Financial Position

Over the last 20 years, PBGC has experienced marked swings in its annual net financial position for its single-employer program (see fig. 3). For example, by fiscal year-end 1990, PBGC experienced a $3.0 billion (in 2011 dollars) accumulated deficit, but by fiscal year-end 2000, PBGC's deficit had shifted to a nearly $12.5 billion surplus (in 2011 dollars), in part due to fewer new claims, higher interest rates used to value liabilities, and investment gains. In recent years, PBGC has again reported growing deficits. Between fiscal year-ends 2008 and 2011, the single-employer program's deficit grew from just over $11 billion (in 2011 dollars) to just over $23 billion. Much of this recent increase in its accumulated deficit was the result of investment losses and declines in interest rates in the wake of the economic downturn and the termination of a relatively small number of very large underfunded plans.

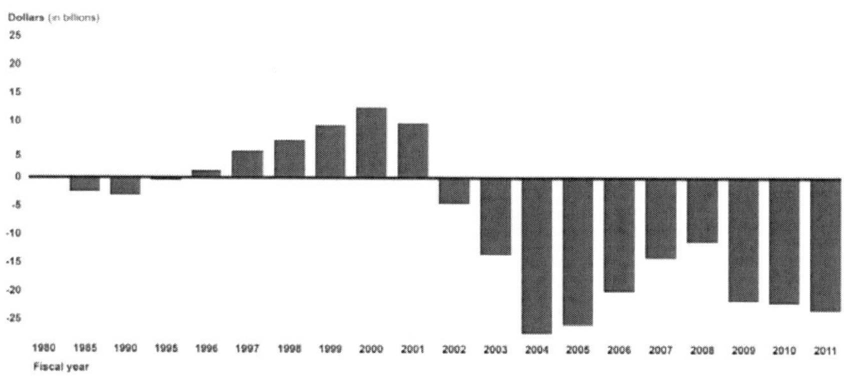

Source: GAO analysis of PBGC data.

Note: Data adjusted for inflation.

Figure 3. PBGC's Surplus/Deficit for the Single-Employer Program, Fiscal Years 1980-2011.

Appendix VI: Overview of Pension Benefit Guaranty Corporation's Pension Insurance Modeling System

In 1998, PBGC began to use its Pension Insurance Modeling System (PIMS) to help the agency better understand and quantify its long-term risk and exposure to loss under different economic conditions and policy alternatives. Much like insurers of catastrophic risk (natural disasters), PBGC is vulnerable to large losses that occur with relatively low probabilities. With these types of insurance, the historic pattern of claims is not an adequate predictor of future experience. Instead, it is more informative to examine the underlying processes that give rise to claims and assess their likelihood of occurring. PIMS is a stochastic (randomly determined) simulation model designed to quantify the amount of risk facing PBGC's two insurance programs. The model does not predict future claims. Rather, by fully exploiting the historic relationships of key economic variables, the model assigns probabilities to various levels of potential claims. PBGC uses this information to estimate its potential future financial positions. PIMS is also used to assess various policy alternatives—such as changes in plan funding requirements or PBGC's premium structure—and their impact on PBGC's financial condition. PIMS is not used to calculate the current deficit. (See appendix V for information on how PBGC calculates its deficit.)

PIMS randomly simulates elements in PBGC's financial statement. The random effects in the simulation are based on measures of the historical volatility in key factors that underlie the pension insurance, including interest rates, stock market returns, and corporate bankruptcy rates. For each year in a simulation, the model randomly selects values for each element and, combining these factors, determines PBGC's financial condition under that scenario. The model generates thousands of multiyear projections of PBGC's future financial condition. The results from the different scenarios are compiled to show how frequently different types of outcomes are simulated. The frequency with which an outcome is simulated (for example, that PBGC attains a surplus in the next 10 years) estimates the likelihood of that outcome's actual occurrence.

Step 1: Modeling the Underlying Mechanics

To project a range of PBGC's possible future financial positions, PIMS must begin by modeling some of the underlying mechanics and relationships that feed into the simulated outcomes. These portions of the model include macroeconomic factors, corporate sponsor behavior, and pension plan behavior.

Macroeconomic Factors

According to PBGC, the most important variables in PIMS are two macroeconomic factors: stock returns and interest rates. Stock returns are modeled to fluctuate in the short-term but revert to a long-term average, so each year's S&P 500 return is equal to 10.4 percent plus a random disturbance. The disturbance is randomly selected to represent the historic distribution of stock returns. Interest rates, unlike stock returns, are correlated over time. To model interest rates, PIMS uses a simple random walk process whereby this year's interest rate equals last year's interest rate plus a random disturbance. Because stock returns are more likely to be high when factors related to the interest rate are falling, PIMS uses historical estimates to correlate the random disturbances that affect stock returns and interest rates.

Plan Sponsor Behavior

For plan sponsors, PIMS models measures of financial health and, from that, the probability of bankruptcy. The measures of financial health include financial ratios (i.e., equity-to-debt and cash flow-to-asset ratios), employment levels, and equity values. Financial ratios are modeled as a regression to long-term averages of these measures, with random disturbances. Employment and equity levels are modeled using a random walk process, and values for both measures are correlated based on their historical relationship. To model plan sponsor bankruptcy, PIMS measures the historical relationship between the probability of bankruptcy and firms' employment levels and financial ratios. These factors, taken together, determine the probability that a sponsor will enter bankruptcy during a given period.

Pension Plan Behavior

To model pension plan behavior, PIMS uses a database with detailed information about a non-representative sample of 450 of the 28,000 plans covered by PBGC. These 450 plans represented about half of PBGC's insurance exposure in the single-employer DB system.[1] The plans in the sample are weighted based on funding ratios to represent all plans insured by PBGC. Plan information in the PIMS database includes asset returns, sponsor contributions, participant composition, and benefit and salary levels.

- *Asset returns.* PIMS uses historical information of individual plans' returns based on correlations with stock returns and interest rates. Each plan's asset returns also has a random element that is not correlated to the simulated economic scenario.

- *Sponsor contributions.* PIMS models sponsor contributions in two different ways: (1) for projecting future claims, sponsors are assumed to make the minimum contribution required by Internal Revenue Code; and (2) for projecting variable-rate premium collections, a higher level of contributions reflects historical data on PBGC premium collections.
- *Participant composition.* PIMS models participant composition by simulating participants' retirement, separation from employment, and death based on actuarial assumptions. In addition, the number of active participants in each plan fluctuates according to the sponsor's total employment level.
- *Benefit and salary levels.* PIMS models benefit level growth as equal to the rate of inflation plus a fixed parameter to represent productivity growth. To model salaries paid, PIMS assumes that salaries grow with age and service to reflect merit and promotion, and average salary levels for a given age and service level grow at the rate of inflation plus productivity growth.

Step 2: Combining Components into Simulated Scenarios

In a simulation, PIMS uses these components of its model to project possible outcomes. PIMS first draws a series of stock returns and interest rates—called an economic scenario—one for each simulated year. Next, plan sponsors and pension plans are all subjected to the economic scenario to determine how they react and, ultimately, how it affects PBGC. To create a distribution of possible future outcomes, PIMS draws 500 unique economic scenarios and runs plan sponsors through each economic scenario 10 times for a total of 5,000 different simulations.

Plan Sponsors' Risk of Bankruptcy

Each plan sponsor is brought through the series of economic scenarios. The model draws new financial ratios and employment levels for each sponsor in each simulated year and, based on that, assigns each sponsor a probability of bankruptcy. PIMS uses this probability to determine whether a sponsor enters bankruptcy during each scenario. To illustrate, PIMS models a sponsor's chances of bankruptcy as a lottery urn filled with balls. If a sponsor has a 1 percent probability of bankruptcy during an economic scenario, its urn contains one ball to represent bankruptcy and 99 balls to represent survival to the next period. PIMS draws a ball from the urn for each of the times a firm is cycled through the model's simulated economic scenarios.[2] A sponsor enters bankruptcy during any simulation where PIMS draws the ball that represents bankruptcy. Plans sponsored by bankrupt sponsors are assumed to present a claim to PBGC if they are less than 80 percent funded. Otherwise a standard termination is assumed.

Pension Plans' Risk of Underfunding

PIMS brings each pension plan through the economic scenario, with equity returns, interest rates, and its sponsor's simulated employment level and plan demographics all affecting the plan's assets and liabilities. By including minimum funding rules to simulations, PIMS calculates possible paths in underfunding within the constraints of existing funding rules. In addition, plan sponsors will be assessed PBGC premiums and make contributions to the plan. For purposes of modeling future claims in PIMS, it is assumed that employers will contribute the minimum required amount each year and that any credit balance remaining when any new funding rules take effect will be used to the maximum extent permitted until the balance is completely depleted.

PBGC's Financial Position and Risk of Loss

Finally, PBGC is brought through the economic scenario. This includes effects on PBGC's existing assets and liabilities from previously terminated plans, both from investment returns and from revaluations of liabilities due to changes in interest rates. The agency also makes benefit payments to trusteed participants and collects premiums from sponsors. To determine premium revenue, PIMS estimates revenue associated with flat-rate premiums (based on each plan's projected participant level) and variable-rate premiums (based on each plan's projected funding level). PBGC may also experience a new claim associated with sponsor bankruptcy. When a plan sponsor enters bankruptcy, PIMS estimates the level of underfunding for benefits that PBGC guaranties; any plan funded at 80 percent or less becomes a claim on PBGC.

To project PBGC's future financial condition, PIMS uses a detailed database of about 450 actual plans, sponsored by about 330 firms, which represent about half of PBGC's insurance exposure in the single-employer DB system measured from the Form 5500 filings. The database includes the plan demographics, plan benefit structure, asset values, liabilities, and actuarial assumptions. It also includes key financial information about the employer sponsoring the plan. The PIMS database contains pension plan information from Schedule B of the Form 5500 (Annual Return/Report of Employee

Benefit Plan). In addition, more recent data available from filings under section 4010 of ERISA[3] is utilized for certain large underfunded plans.

Step 3: Summarizing the Results

In its 2010 exposure report,[4] PBGC estimates that of out of 5,000 simulations, none project that PBGC's single-employer program will run out of money within the next 10 years (fiscal year 2020). In the PIMS projection for the PBGC 2010 Annual Report, 2.5 percent of the simulations project that the program will run out of money by fiscal year 2030. A slight majority of the simulations result in improved or unchanged positions.

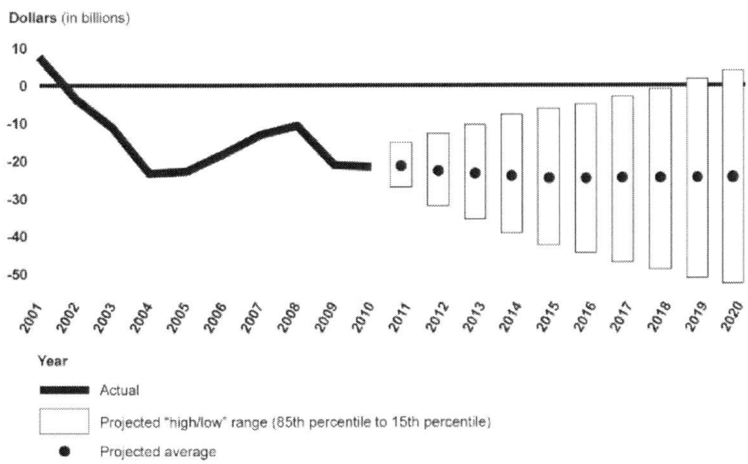

Source: PBGC data.

Note: The projected net financial positions for future fiscal years after 2010 are calculated as present values as of 2010.

Figure 4. PBGC Actual and Projected Net Financial Position for the Single-Employer Program, Fiscal Years 2001-2020.

However, because some simulations result in very large deficits for the program, the average (mean) outcome is a decline in the program's position from a deficit of $21.3 in fiscal year 2011 to a deficit of $24.2 billion (present value as of 2010) by fiscal year 2020 (see fig. 4). PIMS offers a range of probable outcomes, with high and low values calculated for each year. Although PBGC projects a zero percent probability that its single-employer program will be insolvent by the end of fiscal year 2020, as the figure shows, the high and low value estimates—which represent the 85th and 15th percentiles for the projections—ranges from a surplus of $4 billion to a deficit of nearly $53 billion for that fiscal year.[5]

Limitations of PIMS

PIMS is not a predictive model and it does not attempt to anticipate behavioral responses by a company to changed circumstances, such as changes to the premium structure. For example, the model has not been used to anticipate a sponsor's behavioral reaction—such as voluntarily terminating or freezing their plans, or increasing plan funding above the minimum required, or changing plan asset allocation—to an increase in premiums or to the introduction of risk factors to premium rates. Various paths of underfunding can occur in the future, and PIMS does not allow PBGC to know which particular path of underfunding might occur or which particular firms might enter bankruptcy. However, PBGC assumes that the process that generates historical volatility in key variables is reasonably representative of the process that governs future volatility, and that PIMS provides for a reasonable evaluation of the likelihood that various economic scenarios can develop. By modeling real pension plans and incorporating minimum funding rules, PBGC uses PIMS to quantify the likelihood that various levels of exposure can develop under these conditions. In May 2012, PBGC's Inspector General identified internal control deficiencies related to the agency's PIMS model.[6] PBGC's Inspector General reported that the agency published its 2010 exposure report with erroneous and inconsistent results from its PIMS model. Furthermore, the Inspector General reported that PBGC's Policy Research and Analysis Department did not conduct any documented review of the underlying support used for the report and lacks quality control policies to ensure the integrity of reported estimates. The report made several recommendations to ensure the quality of this department's actuarial work products, including establishing policies and procedures to review contractor work performed with PIMS; establishing policies and procedures to retain supporting documentation of work done by department actuaries and actuarial contractors; and developing and documenting a strategic review of the process of creating actuarial reports to identify critical control points to increase quality control. PBGC's response to the Inspector General's findings includes a commitment to strengthening and documenting the quality assurance process, to posting a corrected report on PBGC's website, and to noting the errors in the forthcoming fiscal year 2011 exposure report. Relevant to these deficiencies, Congress also made improvements to PBGC in MAP-21.[7] Under those amendments, PBGC is to contract with an outside agency or organization to conduct an annual review of PIMS, and PBGC officials noted that at their request, the Social Security Administration has agreed to conduct the review. The first reviews will be initiated no later than 3 months after the enactment of the act. Further, PBGC is also required to establish written quality control procedures for modeling and actuarial work done in the Policy Research and Analysis Department, including a record management review to determine records that must be retained. Within two months, PBGC is required to submit a report to Congress detailing a timetable for addressing recommendations from the Inspector General's recent report on the department, which was provided on September 6, 2012.

APPENDIX VII: PLAN SPONSORS AND PENSION EXPERTS INTERVIEWED

Plan Sponsors

We conducted interviews with a small judgmental sample of nine plan sponsors, selected to reflect a range of attributes, including company financial health, plan funded status, size of plan (based on the market value of the plan's assets), number of participants, status of plan (active or frozen), and union involvement.[1]

- Comerica Incorporated, Dallas, Texas (financial services)
- Exelon Corporation, Chicago, Illinois (energy provider)
- General Electric Company, Fairfield, Connecticut (multiple industries)
- Lockheed Martin Corporation, Bethesda, Maryland (aeronautics /electronics)
- R.R. Donnelley & Sons Company, Chicago, Illinois (communications)
- The McClatchy Company, Sacramento, California (publishing)
- Tomkins PLC, London, United Kingdom (engineering/manufacturing)
- TOTAL S.A., Courbevoie, France (energy provider)
- Whirlpool Corporation, Benton Harbor, Michigan (home appliances)

Pension Experts

We also conducted interviews with pension experts reflecting a range of academic, actuarial, business, and labor perspectives from the institutions and organizations listed below.[2]

- American Benefits Council
- AFL-CIO
- American Academy of Actuaries
- American Enterprise Institute
- American Society of Pension Professionals and Actuaries
- Boston University
- Brookings Institution
- Covington & Burling
- Davis and Harman Drexel University
- Employee Benefit Research Institute
- ERISA Industry Committee
- Massachusetts Institute of Technology
- National Institute on Retirement Security
- The New School
- Pennsylvania State University
- Pension Rights Center
- Society of Actuaries
- Towers Watson
- United Auto Workers
- U.S. Chamber of Commerce

Appendix VIII: History of Pension Benefit Guaranty Corporation Premiums for the Single-Employer Program, Fiscal Years 1974 to 2012

For plan years beginning	Flat-rate premium (per participant)	Variable-rate premium (per $1000 of unfunded vested benefits)[b]	Termination premium (per participant per year for 3 years)[b]
1974-1977	$1.00	-	-
1978-1985	2.60	-	-
1986-1987	8.50	-	-
1988-1990	16.00	$6	-

For plan years beginning	Flat-rate premium (per participant)	Variable-rate premium (per $1000 of unfunded vested benefits)b	Termination premium (per participant per year for 3 years)b
1994-2005	19.00	9	-
2006	30.00[a]	9	$1,250
2007	31.00	9	1,250
2008	33.00	9	1,250
2009	34.00	9	1,250
2010-2012	35.00	9	1,250

Source: GAO analysis of PBGC data.

[a] For each plan year beginning after 2006, this amount is adjusted annually based on changes in the national average wage index, as defined in section 209(k)(1) of the Social Security Act, (42 U.S.C. § 409(k)(1)). 29 U.S.C. § 1306(a)(3)(F). The premium rate will not decline even if the national average wage index declines. The adjusted premium rate is rounded to the nearest multiple of $1.

[b] Where dashes are shown, the variable-rate premium and termination premium did not yet exist.

End Notes

[1] Pub. L. No. 93-406, § 4002(a), 88 Stat. 829, 1004 (codified as amended at 29 U.S.C. § 1302(a)).

[2] PBGC administers two separate insurance programs: a single-employer program and a multiemployer program. The single-employer program, comprised of about 25,000 DB plans, insures each plan established and maintained by one employer. The much smaller multiemployer program, comprised of about 1,500 plans, insures plans that are arranged through collective bargaining between one or more labor unions and a group of employers in a particular trade or industry. This report focuses on the challenges facing PBGC's single-employer program.

[3] Generally speaking, a claim occurs when a plan sponsor with an underfunded plan goes bankrupt.

[4] Pub. L. No. 109-280, 120 Stat. 780.

[5] Pub. L. No. 112-141, § 40221, 126 Stat. 404, 850-52 (2012). Although primarily about funding highways, MAP-21 also included several pension-related provisions, requiring changes to the funding rules for DB plan sponsors, strengthening PBGC governance practices, as well as increasing premium rates for DB plans covered by PBGC's single-employer and multiemployer insurance programs. Pub. L. No. 112-141, § 40221, 126 Stat. 404, 846-59 (2012). (See app. I for more information on the pension-related provisions included in MAP-21.)

[6] We did not conduct independent legal analysis to verify the information about PPF's premium framework, but rather relied on a review of publicly available PPF documents and discussions with PPF officials. See appendix IV for a description of the risk factors PPF has incorporated into its premium structure in the UK.

[7] In May 2012, PBGC's Inspector General released a report finding that PIMS lacks key internal controls to ensure the integrity of the model's reported results. See PBGC Office of

Inspector General, *Ensuring the Integrity of Policy Research and Analysis Department's Actuarial Calculations*, PA-12-87 (Washington, D.C.: May 2012).

[8] Pension Benefit Guaranty Corporation, *2010 PBGC Annual Exposure Report.* (Washington, D.C.: November 2011).

[9] 29 U.S.C. §§ 1302(a)(2) and 1361. The guarantied benefit limits for participants in single-employer plans cannot exceed the statutory maximum, adjusted annually, at the time the plan terminates. For 2012, the maximum is $54,000 per year for a person retiring at age 65 with no survivor benefit (that is, a single-life annuity). The maximum is lower for those retiring under age 65 or with a survivor benefit. 29 U.S.C. § 1322(b)(3); 29 C.F.R. § 4022.23 (2012). Other guarantied benefit limits for participants in single-employer plans include the phase-in limit and accrued-at-normal limit. Under the phase-in limit, for any benefit increase implemented through a plan amendment that has been in effect for less than 5 years, only a pro-rata portion can be guarantied. 29 U.S.C. § 1322(b)(1) and (7); 29 C.F.R. § 4022.25 (2012). Under the accrued-at-normal limit, the monthly guarantied benefit cannot be greater than the monthly benefit available at the plan's normal retirement age provided as a straight-life annuity (that is, a periodic payment for the life of the retiree), with no additional payments to survivors. 29 C.F.R. § 4022.21 (2012).

[10] 29 U.S.C. § 1302(d). Prior to the enactment of the PPA, ERISA charged the Secretary of Labor, as the chair of PBGC's board, with administering PBGC. The Secretary has, in turn, historically delegated the responsibility for administering PBGC to an executive director. Since the enactment of PPA, the director has replaced the chair of the board as PBGC administrator. § 411(a), 120 Stat. 935.

[11] We have previously reported concerns regarding PBGC's board, including limitations in its ability to provide policy direction and oversight to PBGC, and the need for the implementation of certain types of reporting requirements—such as congressional notifications and reporting protocols for advisory committees—to ensure effective communication between PBGC and Congress. See GAO, *Pension Benefit Guaranty Corporation: Governance Structure Needs Improvements to Ensure Policy Direction and Oversight*, GAO-07-808 (Washington, D.C.: July 6, 2007) and *Pension Benefit Guaranty Corporation: Improvements Needed to Strengthen Governance Structure and Strategic Management,* GAO-11-182T (Washington, D.C.: Dec. 1, 2010).

[12] § 40231, 126 Stat.853-56.

[13] 29 U.S.C. §§ 1322 and 1322a. The single-employer program insures plans established and maintained by one employer. Single-employer plans can be established unilaterally by the sponsor or through a collective bargaining agreement with a labor union. The multiemployer program insures plans that are arranged through collective bargaining between a labor union and a group of employers in a particular trade or industry. Management and labor representatives must jointly govern multiemployer plans. 29 U.S.C. § 1002(37).

[14] 29 U.S.C. § 1302(a).

[15] 29 U.S.C. § 1341(b). If the sponsor of a single-employer plan meets the statutory requirements for financial distress and the plan does not have sufficient assets to pay promised ("vested accrued") benefits, the plan cannot be terminated as a standard termination. Instead, the plan will be terminated as distress or involuntary termination, and PBGC will likely become the plan's trustee, assuming responsibility for paying benefits to participants as they become due, up to the guarantied benefit limits. 29 U.S.C. § 1341(c). PBGC may initiate an "involuntary" termination if a plan has not met minimum funding standards, a plan will be unable to pay benefits when due, a reportable event has occurred, or the possible long-run

loss to PBGC with respect to a plan may reasonably be expected to increase if the plan is not terminated. 29 U.S.C. § 1342(a).

[16] For example, a pension plan may close to new participants, or a plan may opt to prohibit existing participants from earning pension benefits in the future.

[17] The PPA included provisions to modify funding rules and increase premiums for sponsors of single-employer plans. §§ 101, 102, 111, and 112, and 401 and 405, 120 Stat. 784-809, 820-846, and 922 and 928-29. However, Congress has provided sponsors with funding relief in the last few years and revised some provisions to help mitigate the effects of the recent economic downturn. Worker, Retiree, and Employer Recovery Act of 2008, Pub. L. No. 110-458, §§ 101, 102, 121 and 122, 122 Stat. 5092, 5093-5103, 5113- 14, Preservation of Access to Care for Medicare Beneficiaries and Pension Relief Act of 2010, Pub. L. No. 111-192, tit. II, 124 Stat.1280, 1283-1306, and MAP-21, § 40221, 126 Stat. 850-52.

[18] 29 U.S.C. § 1305(b). Throughout this report we refer to all funds generated through the investment of assets as investment income. For further discussion of PBGC's investment strategy; see GAO, *Pension Benefit Guaranty Corporation: Asset Management Needs Better Stewardship*, GAO-11-271 (Washington, D.C.: June 30, 2011).

[19] PBGC officials noted that where present values are meaningful, such as in calculating PBGC's deficit, it is important to consider PBGC's current financial position in determining the adequacy of future premiums. In addition, they also noted that the adequacy of any premium structure is highly dependent on investment income that (a) can improve PBGC's financial position over long periods if PBGC's assets are expected to earn more than the discount rate on its liabilities, as has been the case; (b) can and has created significant gains and losses in PBGC's financial position due to market fluctuations and the impact on PBGC's and insured plan's asset returns; and (c) cannot reduce the growth of the existing deficit to the extent that liabilities exceed assets.

[20] The value of liabilities is equal to the actuarial present value of projected future benefit payments, which is determined by use of certain assumptions about interest rates, among other things, to adjust the amount of future benefit payments to reflect the time value of money (by discounting) and the probability of payment (by means of decrements, such as for death or retirement). PBGC also includes the estimated liabilities in excess of assets for new claims that it deems probable.

[21] See appendix V for a more detailed description of how PBGC calculates its deficit.

[22] GAO, *Pension Benefit Guaranty Corporation: Long-Term Vulnerabilities Warrant "High Risk"*, GAO-03-1050SP (Washington, D.C.: July 23, 2003); *High-Risk Series: An Update*, GAO-09-271 (Washington, D.C.: January 2009); and *High-Risk Series: An Update*, GAO-11-278 (Washington, D.C.: February 2011), 150-153. Although we designated PBGC's single-employer program as a "high-risk" program in 2003, we first designated PBGC as a high-risk area in 1990, citing taxpayers' exposure to potential losses from the termination of large, underfunded plans. In 1995, we removed PBGC from our list of high-risk areas due to congressional and agency actions that we believed would reduce PBGC's exposure to losses. In 2009, we also designated the multiemployer program as high risk.

[23] Historically under ERISA, PBGC was granted a $100 million line of credit from the federal government. ERISA, § 4005(c), 88 Stat. 1010. Under MAP-21, enacted in July 2012, this line of credit was discontinued. § 40234, 126 Stat. 858.

[24] GAO, *Pension Benefit Guaranty Corporation: Single-Employer Pension Insurance Program Faces Significant Long-Term Risks*, GAO-04-90 (Washington, D.C.: October 29, 2003).

[25] The nearly $2.1 billion in premium revenue in fiscal year 2011 consisted of $1.1 billion in flat-rate premiums and $929 million in variable-rate premiums.

[26] 29 U.S.C. § 1306(a)(3)(A)(1), (E) and (F). A termination premium of $1,250 per participant per year for 3 years generally applies when a single-employer plan terminates in a distress termination under 29 U.S.C. § 1341(c)(2)(B)(ii) or (iii) or in an involuntary termination under 29 U.S.C. § 1342. 29 U.S.C. § 1306(a)(7)(A). However, this premium does not apply in the case of a plan terminated under 29 U.S.C. §§ 1341(c)(2)(B)(ii) or 1342 during the pendency of a bankruptcy reorganization (29 U.S.C. § 1306(7)(b)), or to any plan termination during the pendency of any bankruptcy reorganization filed before October 18, 2005 (Deficit Reduction Act of 2005, Pub. L. No. 109-171, § 8101(b) and (d), 120 Stat. 181-22 and 183 (2006)).

[27] § 40221(b)(3), 126 Stat. 852 (codified at 29 U.S.C. § 1306(a)(3)(E)(i)(II)).

[28] See appendix VIII for a summary of historical PBGC premium rates, 1974 to 2012.

[29] For the purpose of this projection, PBGC assumed that the flat rate would increase each year over the current rate by approximately $1 to account for an annual increase in the wage growth index and that the variable rate would remain the same as current law for the period.

[30] See Steven Boyce and Richard A. Ippolito, "The Cost of Pension Insurance," *The Journal of Risk and Insurance*, vol. 69, no. 2 (2002): 121-170.

[31] PBBC's estimated total unfunded liabilities are based on all plan liabilities, whether vested or not.

[32] See U.S. Congressional Budget Office, *The Risk Exposure of the Pension Benefit Guaranty Corporation* (Washington, D.C.: September 2005).

[33] The uniform premium also does not vary according to sponsor or plan characteristics.

[34] On July 6, 2012, the President signed into law MAP-21, which included provisions calling for rate increases within PBGC's current premium structure for all single-employer plan sponsors insured by PBGC. § 40221, 126 Stat. 446-448 (2012). The act also provided for rate increases for all multiemployer plan sponsors insured by PBGC. Pub. L. No. 112-141, § 40222, 126 Stat. 852-53.

[35] In constructing its model, PBGC selected a sample of plans from its 2010 premium database that had readily available data regarding either the sponsor's credit rating or Dun & Bradstreet score. The resulting sample included 1,114 sponsors of 2,699 DB plans covering 27.5 million participants. The model covered 81 percent of all PBGC-insured participants (33.8 million) in 2010. We validated the model by reviewing the formulas PBGC used to analyze the 2010 premium data and assessed the reliability of the data used in the model. Where we found problems with formulas or other points of information used in the model's analysis, we discussed these issues with PBGC officials and made corrections to their analysis.

[36] For the purpose of its analysis in the premium model, PBGC estimated a combined flat and variable rate on a per participant basis for the hypothetical option to increase rates under the current structure in order to make comparisons to per participant rates under other options. Under the hypothetical option to increase rates under the current structure, PBGC estimated that the combined per participant rate (i.e., the flat rate, plus the amount collected from the variable rate divided by the number of plan participants) ranged from $60 to $4,367. By way of comparison, PBGC calculated that combined premium rates under the structure in place for fiscal year 2010 ranged from $35 per participant to $2,481.

[37] 29 U.S.C. § 1306(a)(3)(E).

[38] Data for fiscal year 2011 were through April 2011.

[39] Two pension experts we spoke with believe that PBGC is not a true insurance program, since it is statutorily required to insure all DB plans. These experts instead believe that this makes PBGC more of a social protection program, providing participants a social safety net by

obligating the payment of pension benefits up to certain limits for underfunded plans that terminate.

[40] The President had also proposed in his September 2011 deficit reduction plan that total PBGC premiums for any plan would not exceed four times the amount payable with respect to the plan for the 2010 plan year, on a per participant basis. Under PBGC's risk-based option, PBGC estimates that 84 percent of the total increase in premium revenue over 2010 levels would be attributable to the increase in the variable rate for sponsors. See Office of Management and Budget, "Living Within Our Means and Investing in the Future, The President's Plan for Economic Growth and Deficit Reduction," (September 2011).

[41] This particular premium design assesses the variable rate portion of the premium— which reflects both plan underfunding and sponsor financial health—on a per participant basis. An alternative would be to assess the variable rate portion as a percentage of the plan's liability—which would reflect the fact that two plans with the same number of participants could have different levels of plan liability, and therefore risk exposure, per participant, because of differences in the level of benefits provided by the plan and in the ages of plan participants.

[42] For more information on FDIC's efforts to tie premiums to the estimated risk a bank poses to the agency, see GAO, *Deposit Insurance: Assessment of Regulators' Use of Prompt Corrective Action Provisions and FDIC's New Deposit Insurance System* GAO-07-242 (Washington, D.C.: Feb. 15, 2007).

[43] The designated reserve ratio is currently set at 2 percent. According to FDIC officials, regulations implemented in 2010 allow the FDIC to set assessment rates at moderate levels when the designated reserve ratio exceeds 1.15 percent and progressively lower assessment rates when the reserve ratio exceeds 2 percent and 2.5 percent.

[44] We did not conduct independent legal analysis to verify the information on UK's DB premium framework, but rather relied on a review of publicly available PPF documents and discussions with PPF officials.

[45] PPF refers to plans as schemes and premiums as levies. For the purpose of this report, we continue to use plans and premiums when discussing PPF's premium framework.

[46] In the UK, the Dun & Bradstreet failure score predicts the likelihood that a company will obtain legal relief from its creditors or cease operations over the next 12-month period. It is presented as a ranking score ranging from 1-100: 1 indicates the highest risk of failure and 100 the lowest level of risk. Businesses with the same failure score have the same risk of failure.

[47] According to PPF officials, the funding position of plans is reported through an exchange system on a consistent basis, as specified in PPF guidance, and transformed to a consistent date by rolling forward the assets and liabilities notified to a consistent date. The exchange is maintained by the UK's Pensions Regulator, the agency responsible for regulating pension plans in the UK. The exchange allows sponsors to upload information about their plans and make premium payments electronically.

[48] PPF's annual revenue target is based on estimates of the funds required to meet certain future financial goals. Beginning in August 2010, PPF has published its funding strategy, which sets out how the agency intends to have the financial resources needed to pay existing levels of compensation to current and future PPF participants and become financially self-sufficient by 2030. For plan year 2012/13, the premium scaling factor is set to scale down risk-based premiums so that together with the plan-based premiums, PPF will collect revenue sufficient to meet its target ($864 million) for the year.

[49] To reduce the impact of short-term volatility in the financial markets, and to ensure that all plans are treated on a consistent basis, for plan year 2012/13, PPF will smooth the value of the assets and liabilities that a plan reports using 5-year financial market averages up to March 30, 2012.

[50] The cap for 2012/13 is 75 basis points (0.75 percent) of smoothed liabilities. Where the risk-based premium calculated using the above formula exceeds 0.75 percent of a plan's liabilities, the cap is applied and the premium is decreased accordingly.

[51] While the premium cap applies only to some plans' risk-based premiums, the multiplier is spread across all plans' plan-based premiums to help meet PPF's revenue target. PPF contends that this approach also makes the necessary cross-subsidy in the plan-based premium more transparent as it ends the practice of scaling up risk-based premiums to cover the cost of capping. In essence, PPF is minimizing the amount of cross-subsidization in the plan-based premium by limiting it to only cover premiums lost via the capping on risk-based premiums. In contrast, in the previous plan year (2011/12), a multiplier was applied to every plan so that plan-based premiums accounted for an estimated 20 percent of the total pension protection premium estimate for the year.

[52] PPF defines self-sufficiency as a level of assets 10 percent in excess of its liabilities. In addition to being fully funded, PPF's goal is to eliminate its exposure to interest rate fluctuation, inflation, and other market risks. PPF also wants to build a reserve to further protect itself against future claims and the impact of members living longer than it estimates. Most recently, PPF's latest assessments show that the probability of achieving self-sufficiency measured on its base case has improved from 83 percent in March 2010 to 87 percent in March 2011.

[53] To help reduce volatility for plan sponsors, PPF's risk-based premium is now fixed for 3 years. Beginning with the 2012/13 plan year, PPF revised its funding strategy to reflect a "bottom up" approach in which risk factor parameters will be fixed for 3 years and, ideally, remain stable between each 3-year review. Under this approach, PPF intends to keep the risk-based premium scaling factor and the plan-based multiplier fixed for 3 years—a sponsor's risk-based premium will only change if its risk level changes. Previous to plan year 2012/13, PPF's model reflected a "top down" approach in which PPF would decide upon the premium that it deemed appropriate in a given year, and then set the premium parameters accordingly on an annual basis.

[54] A plan freeze is an amendment to the plan to limit some or all future pension accruals for some or all of the plan participants. For example, a pension plan may close to new participants, or a plan may opt to prohibit existing participants from earning pension benefits in the future.

[55] As of 2008, larger sponsors, those with 10,000 or more total participants, were significantly less likely than smaller sponsors to have implemented a hard freeze. Similarly, firms with some or all plans subject to collective bargaining are significantly less likely to implement hard freezes than sponsors with no plans subject to collective bargaining. See GAO, *Defined Benefit Pensions: Plan Freezes Affect Millions of Participants and May Pose Retirement Income Challenges*, GAO-08-817 (Washington, D.C.: July 21, 2008).

[56] Towers Watson conducted the survey from October 2011 to December 2011 and included responses from 424 DB plan sponsors at midsize and large organizations. Respondents were asked about changes to their retirement plans over the past 10 years, their motivations behind those changes and their future retirement offerings. See Towers Watson, *Pensions in Transition: Retirement Plan Changes and Employer Motivations* (New York, N.Y.: May 2012).

[57] While higher premiums were not cited as a reason to freeze or terminate a plan, lower premiums were cited as a potential reason to reopen a plan after it had been frozen. *Ibid.*

[58] According to PBGC's analysis of Bureau of Labor Statistics data, premiums account for about 1 cent per hour of total average compensation costs. This analysis was based on data that indicated that, on average, private industry employers spend approximately 3.6 percent of total compensation costs on retirement and savings expenses, and of this, PBGC premiums generally account for approximately 3.4 percent of total pension costs. However, PBGC's analysis does not take into account that only about 10 percent of private companies offer access to DB plans. A more accurate calculation would need to reflect the cost of premiums compared to compensation costs among just those firms offering DB plans, but the Bureau of Labor Statistics does not provide a breakdown of data to allow such an analysis.

[59] Our previous work on the topic noted that plan freezes and terminations may impact participants' retirement security by reducing future benefits, though this may be somewhat or entirely offset by increases in other benefits or a replacement retirement-savings plan. Additionally, under a plan termination, it takes PBGC about 3 years, on average, to complete the benefit determination process and provide participants their finalized benefit amounts. Long delays and uncertainty over final benefit amounts in a plan termination make it difficult for workers to plan for retirement, and for retirees who have come to depend on a certain level of monthly income. See GAO-08-817 and GAO, *Pension Benefit Guaranty Corporation: Workers and Retirees Experience Delays and Uncertainty when Underfunded Plans Are Terminated,* GAO10-181T (Washington, D.C.: Oct. 29, 2009).

[60] A hard freeze—the most common type of freeze—occurs when all future benefit accruals cease. PBGC officials noted that freezes have occurred disproportionately in smaller plans and that a more accurate metric may be the number of workers affected by a freeze. According to PBGC, just over 75 percent of all active employees participating in PBGC-insured single-employer DB plans are still accruing benefits and are in plans that still cover new employees, indicating that less than 25 percent are in plans that have been affected by a freeze.

[61] However, voluntary standard plan terminations can be costly, as plan sponsors must fully fund all benefits, either by distributing lump-sum payments (to the extent allowed under the plan and elected by participants) or by purchasing annuities to secure participants' benefits into the future. 29 U.S.C. § 1341(b). An underfunded plan cannot be terminated unless the sponsor demonstrates it cannot fund the plan, usually through a bankruptcy proceeding. Thus, when a healthy sponsor terminates an underfunded plan, it first must fully fund the plan prior to termination. When PBGC initiates the termination of a plan, it is because it determines the sponsor will be unable to fund the plan, and it intervenes to protect participants' benefits.

[62] At the same time, PBGC officials noted that in 2010, standard terminations were just about 5 percent lower than the average of 1369 standard terminations for the previous 10 years. PBGC officials also indicated that on average, these plans covered about 80 participants, and of those 1.2 million participants, about half were workers.

[63] The Towers Watson study also found that larger DB plan sponsors are less likely to move away from a DB design than their smaller counterparts and that certain industries (e.g., utilities, health care) are more likely to depend on DB benefits as a vital component of reward packages to attract and retain skilled workers.

[64] As noted earlier, under MAP-21, per participant premium rates are capped at no more than $400 beginning in 2013. Similarly, under the President's deficit reduction proposal, per

participant rates for premiums are capped at no more than four times the rates paid in plan year 2010.

[65] During the recent economic downturn and current economic situation, Congress took similar steps to mitigate the effects of the PPA provisions requiring increased contributions to underfunded plans, allowing sponsors to amortize increases to their contributions over a longer period, postponing implementation of the increased funding requirements for some firms, and averaging market interest rates over a 25-year period to provide relief against the current low interest rate environment. Preservation of Access to Care for Medicare Beneficiaries and Pension Relief Act of 2010, Pub. L. No. 111-192, 124 Stat. 1280,1283-1306, §§ 201-211; and Worker, Retiree, and Employer Recovery Act of 2008, Pub. L. No. 110-458, §§ 101, 102, 121 and 122, 122 Stat. 5092, 5093-5103, 5113-14, and MAP-21, § 40221, 126 Stat. 850-52.

[66] In 2006, FDIC officials noted that the number of institutions in this highest category is small and thus the trade-off between lower premiums for troubled institutions and potentially larger losses for FDIC later would not be significant. See GAO-07-242.

[67] As noted earlier, to help address such concerns, Congress included provisions in MAP-21 to limit the extent of increases in the variable-rate premium. The administration has also proposed limiting the extent of increases by setting a maximum per participant limit to the total amount of a sponsor's increase under a more risk-based premium structure.

[68] See also, American Academy of Actuaries, *Examining the PBGC Premium Structure*, (Washington, D.C.: April 2012). This issue brief describes how PBGC costs could be divided into two distinct categories: (1) going-forward costs, which are associated with the risks of ongoing coverage by PBGC; and (2) past costs, which are associated with existing or imminent claims on PBGC for terminated plans.

[69] PBGC officials noted, however, that commercial measures, such as a company's credit ratings, have been used to estimate the risk of default for individual companies for over a century. Information on creditworthiness on public companies is readily available, and credit scores on private companies are available for purchase from entities such as Dun & Bradstreet.

[70] They believe that the artificially low interest rates following the economic downturn of 2008 have, in turn, artificially inflated PBGC's deficit. Instead of using annuity prices to set interest rates for valuing its future liabilities, these advocates believe it would be more accurate to use a "dollar cost averaging" approach that would set interest rates looking forward over 30 years based on historical interest rates over the last 30 years—much like the approach Congress took in changing funding requirements governing interest rates for DB plans recently in MAP-21, § 40211, 126 Stat. 846-50. For further details on how PBGC calculates its deficit, see appendix V.

[71] 29 U.S.C. §§ 1021(b)(1) and 1023.

[72] 29 U.S.C. § 1310. Specifically, plan sponsors and members of its controlled group are required to report financial and actuarial information to PBGC for plans if the (1) the funding target at the end of the preceding plan year is less than 80 percent, (2) certain conditions for imposition of a lien have been met, or (3) minimum funding waivers in excess of $1 million have been granted with respect to any plan maintained by a sponsor or member of its controlled group, and any portion is still outstanding.

[73] Pub. L. No. 109-280, § 505(a), 120 Stat. 946.

[74] According to PBGC's fact sheet on the program, the Early Warning Program identifies potential business transactions that could jeopardize the pension insurance program, and PBGC works with plans sponsors to negotiate additional contributions or security (which may include letters of credit or financial guaranties) for underfunded pensions within the

context of the transaction. PBGC states that it will work with the company to tailor a settlement that is appropriate to the business transaction and financially feasible for the company.

[75] Pursuant to the Dodd-Frank Wall Street Reform and Consumer Protection Act, federal agencies are to review their regulations and remove any reference to or requirement of reliance on credit ratings and substitute other appropriate standards of creditworthiness. Pub. L. No. 111-203, § 939A, 124 Stat. 1376, 1887 (2010). Thus, PBGC would be required to establish its own standard of creditworthiness rather than use credit ratings to assess the risk of plan sponsors in its premium structure.

[76] The exchange is maintained by The Pensions Regulator, the agency responsible for regulating pension plans in the UK. The exchange enables sponsors to upload information about their plans and make premium payments electronically. The Pensions Regulator works closely with PPF to monitor high-risk plans, minimize claims, and ensure that employers do not take advantage of the insurance provided by PPF.

[77] The Dun & Bradstreet failure score is designed to predict the likelihood that a company will cease operations without paying all creditors over the next 12 months. This includes the onset of failure such as a meeting of creditors, administrator appointments, bankruptcy, receiver appointments, petitions for winding-up and other legal events.

[78] Fiona Stewart and Juan Yermo, "Pension Fund Governance: Challenges and Potential Solutions," *OECD Working Papers on Insurance and Private Pensions,* no. 18. (OECD publishing, Paris, France: June 2008.)

[79] 29 U.S.C. § 1306(a)(3)(A)(i), (E) and (F).

[80] The President's deficit reduction proposal to incorporate additional risk factors into the PBGC premium structure included a provision that would expressly provide for any regulation incorporating risk factors to be subject to congressional review under section 251 of the Contract with America Act of 1996, commonly referred to as the Congressional Review Act (Review Act). Pub. L. No. 104-121, § 251, 110 Stat. 847, 868-74 (codified at 5 U.S.C. §§ 801-805). Under the Review Act, federal agencies promulgating a major rule must submit a copy to GAO and both houses of Congress before it can take effect and Congress may enact a joint resolution of disapproval that is sent to the President, becoming law if he signs it. We report to the Congress on each major rule, summarizing and assessing the procedural steps taken by the federal agencies in promulgating them. Moreover, Congress always has the option of seeking to overrule any regulation through the usual legislative process.

[81] § 40231(a)(2) and (c), 126 Stat. 854-56 (codified at 29 U.S.C. § 1302(e) and (k)). 82§ 40232, 126 Stat. 857.

[83] § 40231(f), 126 Stat. 855-56.

[84] § 40231(b), 126 Stat. 854-55 (codified at 29 U.S.C. § 1302j).

[85] In GAO-07-808, we recommended that PBGC's board should (1) establish formal guidelines that articulate the authorities of the board members, their respective departments, and PBGC's Director and (2) PBGC's board should establish policies, procedures, and mechanisms for providing oversight of PBGC that are consistent with corporate governance guidelines. These recommendations have been implemented. For example, PBGC promulgated a final rule revising the board's bylaws to specifically delineate roles and responsibilities of involved parties. 73 Fed. Reg. 29,985 (May 23, 2008). However, some of our more recent work shows that while the board has been meeting more often during the last few years compared to prior years, its members still have little time to devote to PBGC. See GAO-11-182T.

[86] GAO, *21st Century Challenges: Reexamining the Base of the Federal Government*, GAO-05-325SP (Washington, D.C.: February 2005).

[87] Similarly, the President's recent proposal on deficit reduction called for the PBGC board to consult with individuals or organizations representing the interest of employees, plan sponsors, and the general public in designing a more risk-based premium structure.

[88] Among the academic peer reviews of PIMS, most notable is the PIMS Technical Review Panel in November 1996 (sponsored by the Pension Research Council at the Wharton School, University of Pennsylvania). More recently, the Society of Actuaries, used PIMS to prepare a report on pension contributions, published in 2011. PBGC officials also noted that in 2003, PIMS was reviewed by a major investment bank, which was tasked by PBGC with quantifying the value of the PBGC put. Initially, the bank's analytic team planned to use its own models to perform this analysis. However, after reviewing PIMS and determining that PIMS produced results consistent with their models, the lead consultant decided to use PIMS for the project rather than their own models.

[89] Specifically, the Inspector General found that PBGC had published erroneous and inconsistent results in its 2010 exposure report and that PBGC's Policy Research and Analysis Department failed to conduct documented reviews of the underlying support used for the report and lacked quality control policies to ensure the integrity of reported estimates. See PBGC Office of Inspector General, *Ensuring the Integrity of Policy Research and Analysis Department's Actuarial Calculations*, PA-12-87 (Washington, D.C.: May 2012). For further details, see appendix VI.

[90] Our prior work has noted that the ultimate success of a major policy change—such as the redesign of PBGC's statutory premium structure—depends, in part, on having reliable data and credible analysis to provide a compelling rationale for the proposed change. See GAO-05-325SP.

[91] The President's deficit reduction proposal included safeguards similar to the suggestions outlined here. See Office of Management and Budget, "Living Within Our Means and Investing in the Future, The President's Plan for Economic Growth and Deficit Reduction," (September 2011).

[92] The President's 2013 budget proposal to incorporate additional risk into the PBGC premium structure would prohibit publicly disclosing information used to determine premiums for plan sponsors, and PBGC already protects confidential information.

[93] In previous work, we found that for policy reconsideration efforts of this scale, success depends, in part, on including a clear and transparent process for engaging the broader public in the debate over recommended changes. See GAO-05-325SP.

[94] According to PPF's website, plan sponsors have 28 days to appeal their premium invoice. If a plan sponsor believes its failure score is inaccurate, they are instructed to contact Dun & Bradstreet directly.

[95] This includes the number of appeals directed to PPF. Total number of appeals, including those relating to the Dun & Bradstreet failure score, was 1,500 in 2006/7 and 560 in 2011/12.

[96] This figure reflects the number of PPF-insured plans as of March 31, 2011, the most recently available data.

End Notes for Appendix I

[1] Pub. L. No. 112-141, 125 Stat. 405 (2012). The legislation was enacted primarily to authorize funds for highways, highway safety programs, transit programs and for other purposes.

[2] 29 U.S.C. § 1305.

End Notes for Appendix II

[1] The President also suggested various more specific ideas for changing PBGC's premium structure in his deficit reduction plan. See Office of Management and Budget, "Living Within Our Means and Investing in the Future, The President's Plan for Economic Growth and Deficit Reduction," (September 2011). For example, in this plan, the President called for the PBGC board to consult with individuals or organizations representing the interest of employees, plan sponsors, and the general public in designing a more risk-based premium structure, and specified that total PBGC premiums for any plan would not exceed four times the amount payable with respect to the plan for the 2010 plan year, on a per participant basis.

[2] To estimate the flat-rate premium for the single-employer program for fiscal years 2013 to 2022, PBGC projected that the total participant count in its insured DB plans in this program would remain unchanged. However, PBGC's projection on the level of plan participants over the period stands in contrast to a decline in participants that PBGC has reported beginning in fiscal year 2005. We estimate that on average, participant levels have declined by about a quarter percentage point each year since 2005. Using a higher projected participant count would tend to overstate revenues for the period based on a per participant premium.

[3] PBGC estimates that unfunded vested benefit levels would decrease from nearly $283 billion in fiscal year 2013 to just over $24 billion by fiscal year 2019, remaining close to that level for the remainder of the period. Based on this assumption, PBGC projects that even with rate increases proposed under the President's budget, annual revenues from the variable rate will decrease from $2.2 billion in fiscal year 2013 to $1.7 billion in fiscal year 2022. The actual level of unfunded vested benefits in future years would depend on, among other factors, capital market factors such as stock market returns. Changes in PBGC's assumptions about unfunded vested benefit levels could significantly affect the amount of revenue estimated to be collected through the variable rate.

[4] PBGC uses PIMS to estimate future underfunding under current and future funding rules as a function of a variety of economic parameters. PIMS models the effect of the PPA funding requirements and establishes a baseline for equity returns and interest rates over this period for the underfunding projection. See appendix VI for a description of PIMS.

[5] Pub. L. No. 109-280, §§ 101, 102, 111, and 112, 120 Stat. 784-809 and 820-846. PPA introduced new funding requirements for single-employer DB plans beginning in 2008. It requires plan funding to be equal to 100 percent of the plan's liabilities (these PPA funding target liabilities are not calculated using the same assumptions and methods as the liabilities to determine unfunded vested benefits for purposes of determining variable-rate premiums). The 100 percent funding target is phased in at 92 percent in 2008, 94 percent in 2009, 96 percent in 2010, and 100 percent in 2011 and later years. Any unfunded liability will have to be amortized—paid with interest—over 7 years.

[6] See Pension Benefit Guaranty Corporation Office of Inspector General, *Ensuring the Integrity of Policy Research and Analysis Department's Actuarial Calculations* (Washington, D.C.: May 2012).

End Notes for Appendix IV

[1] PPF refers to plans as schemes and premiums as levies. For the purpose of this report, we continue to use plans and premiums when discussing PPF's premium framework.
[2] We did not conduct independent legal analysis to verify the information in this section of the report but rather relied on a review of publicly available PPF documents and discussions with PPF officials.
[3] The 10 percent margin is to cover the risk of longevity improvements greater than what PPF describes as its best estimate, and also the residual risk of future claims. The year 2030 is chosen as being the time at which the level of risk from future insolvencies is projected to be relatively low compared with the size of PPF.
[4] This was discussed in more detail on pages 22-26 and 40-41 of this report.

End Notes for Appendix V

[1] 29 U.S.C. § 1308.
[2] Plans of companies with credit ratings below investment grade and multiemployer plans that may require future financial assistance are classified as "reasonably possible" terminations, rather than "probable" terminations. Although PBGC uses the estimates for reasonably possible plan terminations to assist with understanding the agency's future financial condition, these estimates are not included in PBGC's calculation of its deficit.
[3] Mark to market is the practice of basing values on current market prices.
[4] In addition to the present value of future benefits calculated for the single-employer program, PBGC values the liabilities for the multiemployer program by calculating the present value of estimated nonrecoverable future financial assistance—that is, estimated nonrecoverable payments to be provided in the future to multiemployer plans that are not able to meet their benefit obligations.
[5] A single-premium nonparticipating group annuity is a contract between an insured entity, such as a plan sponsor, and an insurance company that transfers pension obligations from the plan sponsor or other insured entity to the insurance company, in return for a one-time payment to the insurance company. The insurance company thereby takes on the investment risk, longevity risk, and other risks inherent in pension obligations.
[6] GAO has reported that other than the survey conducted for PBGC, no mechanism exists to collect information on actual group annuity purchase rates. Compared to other alternatives, the PBGC interest rate factors may have the most direct connection to the group annuity market, but PBGC factors are less transparent than other, more direct market-determined alternatives, such as published, high-quality bond interest rates. Such long term bond rates may track changes in group annuity rates over time, but their proximity to group annuity rates is also uncertain. For example, a high-quality long-term bond interest rate may need to be adjusted downward to better reflect the level of group annuity purchase rates. GAO,

Pension Benefit Guaranty Corporation: Single-Employer Pension Insurance Program Faces Significant Long-Term Risks, GAO-03-873T (Washington, D.C.: Sept. 4, 2003). PBGC officials noted that they recently had analyzed the relationship between group annuity rates and long term corporate bond rates and found that there was only a low correlation (0.377 with an r-square of 0.142) between the two over an 8-year observation period from December 2000 to September 2008.

[7] These rates—also known as discount rates—effectively form a two-segment yield curve where cash flows that occur during the initial period are discounted by the "select" interest rate and those occurring after the initial period are discounted by the "ultimate" interest rate. For more on these rates see http://www.pbgc.gov/prac/interest.html.

[8] PBGC recently changed the actuarial assumptions on participant mortality it uses to estimate present value of future benefits. For September 30, 2010, PBGC reported using the 1994 Group Annuity Mortality 94 Static Table set forward 1 year, projected 26 years to 2020 using scale AA. Based on a 2011 study of PBGC's participant mortality, PBGC reported adopting new healthy lives mortality tables for the June 30, 2011, and subsequent valuations. For June 30, 2011, PBGC used the Retirement Plan-2000 Combined Healthy (RP-2000 CH) Male and Female Tables, each set back 1 year and projected 21 years to 2021 using Scale AA. The number of years that PBGC projects the mortality table reflects the number of years from the 2000 base year of the table to the end of the fiscal year (11 years in fiscal year 2011) plus PBGC's calculated duration of its liabilities (10 years in fiscal year 2011). PBGC reported that the study also recommended changes in the mortality assumptions for disabled lives which will also be implemented in the June 30, 2011, and subsequent valuations.

[9] Annuity prices are based on both underlying interest rate and mortality assumptions. When greater longevity is assumed, a higher interest assumption is then needed to produce annuity rates that match those in the American Council of Life Insurers survey.

[10] The 135 plans fall into three categories—plans currently receiving financial assistance; plans that have terminated but have not yet started receiving financial assistance from PBGC; and ongoing plans (not terminated) that the corporation expects will require financial assistance in the future.

[11] PBGC does not provide assistance for the full amount of these multiemployer plans' liabilities, and not all of PBGC's financial assistance to multiemployer plans is nonrecoverable. But, as we have reported previously, only 1 of the 62 plans that received PBGC financial assistance between 1981 and 2009 had repaid its loan as of 2010. See GAO, *Private Pensions: Changes Needed to Better Protect Multiemployer Pension Benefits,* GAO-11-79 (Washington, D.C.: Oct. 18, 2010).

End Notes for Appendix VI

[1] As measured by Form 5500 filings.

[2] A typical simulation consists of 5,000 different scenarios (500 unique economic scenarios, which PBGC and each plan and sponsor experience 10 times).

[3] 29 U.S.C. § 1310.

[4] Pension Benefit Guaranty Corporation, *2010 PBGC Annual Exposure Report.* (Washington, D.C.: November 2011).

[5] The mean projection for the single-employer program is based on a range of possible outcomes. For example, while the set of *all* single-employer results for this period includes "tail" financial positions from a surplus of $55 billion to a deficit of $157 billion, the difference between the projection's high and low values ranges from a $4.0 billion surplus to a $52.5 billion deficit, significantly less than the full range.

[6] Pension Benefit Guaranty Corporation Office of Inspector General, *Ensuring the Integrity of Policy Research and Analysis Department's Actuarial Calculations* (Washington, D.C.: May 2012).

[7] Pub. L. No. 112-141, § 40233, 126 Stat. 857-58, and S. Rep. No. 112-557, at 664 (2012).

End Notes for Appendix VII

[1] To assist in identifying our sample of plan sponsors to be interviewed, we requested a random list of 180 plans from PBGC with certain descriptive information about each of the plans. According to PBGC, the spreadsheet of 180 plans they provided was randomly selected from a listing of all plans in PBGC's 2010 premium database that had readily available data regarding either the sponsor's credit rating for publicly traded companies or Dun & Bradstreet's score for private companies. PBGC officials said they sorted the list of plans in alphabetical order by company and then selected every 15th row to create the random sample of plans. PBGC provided information on company financial health and each plan's funded status, number of participants, market value of assets, and whether the plan was frozen or partially frozen. We added information on union involvement based on what we could discern from the plan names. We then selected an initial list of 18 plans, and another back-up list of 18 plans, that represented an array of characteristics for potential interviews. We were ultimately able to complete interviews with nine sponsors, listed here.

[2] To identify experts to contact, we began with the list of participants from a GAO forum held in 2005, and updated the list with suggestions from agency officials. See GAO, *Highlights of a GAO Forum: The Future of the Defined Benefit System and the Pension Benefit Guaranty Corporation*, GAO-05-578SP (Washington, D.C.: June 2005).

In: Pension Benefit Guaranty Corporation ISBN: 978-1-62808-107-7
Editor: Stan Dupont

Chapter 3

THE PENSION BENEFIT GUARANTY CORPORATION AND SINGLE-EMPLOYER PLAN TERMINATIONS*

Jennifer Staman and Erika K. Lunder

SUMMARY

Recent economic conditions have generated attention with respect to the Pension Benefit Guaranty Corporation (PBGC) and defined benefit pension plans, including the process for terminating plans. The Employee Retirement Income Security Act (ERISA) regulates plan terminations. It provides for three types of single-employer plan terminations—standard, distress, and involuntary—and imposes different responsibilities on the PBGC for each type.

A standard termination occurs when a plan administrator decides to terminate a plan that has assets sufficient to meet its benefit liabilities. The PBGC's involvement in a standard termination is minimal, with its role basically limited to confirming all legal requirements have been met. In a standard termination, the plan sponsor has no further liability to the PBGC or plan participants. The sponsor may be able to recapture any assets remaining after participants have received their share, although the reversion may be subject to tax.

---

* This is an edited, reformatted and augmented version of a Congressional Research Service publication, CRS Report for Congress RS22624, from www.crs.gov, prepared for Members and Committees of Congress, dated September 1, 2011.

A distress termination occurs when a plan administrator seeks to terminate a plan that does not have sufficient assets to cover all the benefits owed to plan participants and beneficiaries. The PBGC is responsible for ensuring that all criteria for termination have been met, as well as for determining whether the plan's assets are sufficient to pay the guarantied benefits and/or meet all benefit liabilities. Meanwhile, the plan sponsor and members of its controlled group are jointly and severally liable to the PBGC for the amount that the benefit liabilities exceed plan assets, with interest, at termination.

An involuntary termination occurs when the PBGC decides a plan should be terminated. The agency must initiate termination proceedings once it determines a plan does not have assets available to pay benefits currently due. It may seek termination under certain circumstances, including the plan has not met the minimum funding requirements; the plan will not be able to pay benefits when due; or the long-run loss to the PBGC may be expected to increase unreasonably if the plan is not terminated. In an involuntary termination, the sponsor and controlled group are jointly and severally liable to the PBGC for the unfunded liabilities.

The PBGC is broadly authorized to make any investigation it deems necessary to enforce ERISA and may assess a penalty against anyone who fails to provide a required notice or other material information. In addition, plan participants, beneficiaries, fiduciaries, and sponsors who are adversely affected by an action of another that violates the termination provisions may file suit in U.S. district court to enjoin the action or obtain other equitable relief. Employee organizations representing affected participants and beneficiaries are also able to file a claim, and the PBGC has the right to intervene in any action.

Finally, if the PBGC determines that a plan should not be terminated, it may stop the termination proceedings and restore the plan. It even has the authority to restore a terminated plan.

INTRODUCTION

Due to the recent economic decline, there has been concern about the pensions of employees if the companies offering these pensions were to fail. The Employee Retirement Income Security Act of 1974 (ERISA), which provides a comprehensive federal scheme for the regulation of pension and other employee benefit plans, includes a plan termination insurance program for defined benefit pension plans.[1] Various types of pension plans are not covered by the insurance program, including defined contribution plans (individual account plans),[2] government plans, and church plans.[3] The insurance program distinguishes between single-employer plans and multiemployer plans (i.e., collectively bargained plans to which more than one company makes contributions). This report discusses only the termination of single-employer plans.

The insurance program is administered by the Pension Benefit Guaranty Corporation (PBGC). The PBGC has two primary responsibilities. First, it oversees plan terminations, which is the focus of this report. Second, the PBGC pays the guarantied benefits of terminated plans, subject to statutory limitations. This report provides an overview of the three types of plan terminations and the PBGC's role in each type of termination. The report also provides a brief overview of the liability of an employer following a plan termination, enforcement and penalties relating to the plan termination provisions, and the ability of the PBGC to restore a plan.

TYPES OF TERMINATIONS

ERISA provides for three types of single-employer plan terminations: standard, distress, and involuntary. The plan administrator initiates a standard or distress termination, whereas the PBGC initiates an involuntary termination.

Standard Termination

A standard termination occurs when a plan administrator decides to terminate a plan that has assets sufficient to meet its benefit liabilities.[4] The plan administrator initiates the termination by giving written notice to each affected party[5] of the intent to terminate the plan between 60 and 90 days in advance of the proposed termination date.[6] He or she must then report information about the plan to the PBGC, including a certification by an enrolled actuary that the plan's assets are sufficient to meet all benefit liabilities.[7] The plan administrator is also responsible for informing the plan participants and beneficiaries of the benefits due them, as well as information used in determining benefit liabilities.[8]

The PBGC's involvement in a standard termination is minimal, and its role is basically to confirm that the above requirements have been met. Upon receiving the plan information, the PBGC generally has 60 days to review it and either approve the termination or send out a notice of noncompliance.[9] If the PBGC determines the requirements have been met, the termination proceeds. The plan administrator then distributes the plan's assets to participants and beneficiaries by purchasing annuities from a commercial insurer or by other permissible means.[10] If there are missing participants, the plan administrator may, after a diligent search, purchase an annuity for these individuals or transfer their distributions to the PBGC, which will hold them until the participants are found.[11] The plan administrator's final action is to certify to the PBGC that the assets have been distributed,[12] and the plan is terminated.

Distress Termination

A distress termination occurs when a plan administrator seeks to terminate a plan that does not have sufficient assets to cover all the benefits owed to plan participants and beneficiaries.[13] The plan may be terminated only if certain criteria are met, such as if its contributing sponsor, or a member of the sponsor's controlled group[14] (1) has filed (or has had filed against such person) a petition for liquidation or reorganization in bankruptcy or insolvency proceedings,[15] and certain other requirements have been met, or (2) has demonstrated that termination is required to enable payment of debts while staying in business or to avoid unreasonably burdensome pension costs caused by a declining workforce.[16]

In order to initiate a distress termination, a plan administrator must give written notice of an intent to terminate the plan to each affected party, including the PBGC, at least 60 days and (except with PBGC approval) not more than 90 days before the proposed termination date.[17] After the notice of intent is submitted to affected parties, the plan administrator must submit certain additional information to the PBGC, which may include a certification by an enrolled actuary regarding the amount of the current value of the assets of the plan, the actuarial present value of the benefit liabilities under the plan, and whether the plan is sufficient to pay benefit liabilities.[18] Based on this information, the PBGC determines whether the distress termination criteria are met (or whether the PBGC is unable to make such a determination) and must notify the plan administrator of its finding as soon as practicable.[19]

If the distress criteria have not been met, the plan continues to operate. If the criteria are met, the PBGC must then determine whether the plan's assets are sufficient to pay the benefits guarantied by the PBGC and/or meet all benefit liabilities. These amounts may be different because, as mentioned, the benefits guarantied by the PBGC under the plan insurance termination program are subject to statutory limitations; therefore, the benefit liabilities owed under the plan may exceed the benefits guarantied by the PBGC. If the PBGC determines that the plan's assets are sufficient to pay benefit liabilities, a plan administrator must carry out termination of the plan under the procedures of a standard termination, and take additional action if necessary.[20] Similarly, if the PBGC determines that a plan has sufficient assets to cover guarantied benefits, but not benefit liabilities, the plan administrator will be required to distribute plan assets as with a standard termination, certify to the PBGC that the distribution has occurred, and take other actions as necessary to terminate the plan.[21]

If the plan's assets are not sufficient to pay the guarantied benefits, the PBGC must commence involuntary termination proceedings (discussed below).[22] If the plan administrator discovers during the distribution that the plan's assets are not sufficient to cover benefits, he or she must notify the PBGC, which may then be required to initiate an involuntary termination.[23] If there are missing participants, the plan administrator may purchase an annuity for these individuals, or transfer their distributions to the PBGC after a diligent search.[24]

Involuntary Termination

An involuntary termination occurs when the PBGC decides a plan should be terminated.[25] The PBGC must initiate termination proceedings once it determines a plan does not have assets available to pay benefits currently due. The PBGC may seek to terminate a plan if

- the plan has not met the minimum funding requirements or the plan has been notified by the Treasury Secretary that a notice of deficiency concerning the initial tax on a funding deficiency has been mailed;
- the plan will not be able to pay benefits when due;
- a distribution of at least $10,000 has been made to a participant who is a substantial owner of the sponsoring company and, immediately after the distribution, the plan has unfunded nonforfeitable benefits; or
- the long-run loss to the PBGC may reasonably be expected to increase unreasonably if the plan is not terminated.[26]

A trustee, who may be the PBGC, may be appointed to administer the plan until it is ordered to be terminated.[27] The trustee may be appointed by a U.S.

district court upon petition by the PBGC or plan administrator, or the PBGC and plan administrator may agree to the appointment without court involvement. Once appointed, the trustee is responsible for the plan's administration, including management of the plan's assets.[28]

After the PBGC has given notice to the plan administrator, the plan may be terminated in one of two ways. First, the PBGC may file a petition with the U.S. district court for a ruling that the plan must be terminated to protect the participants' interests, to avoid an unreasonable deterioration of the plan's financial condition, or to avoid an unreasonable increase in the PBGC's liability.[29] If a trustee has been appointed, he or she may intervene in the proceeding.

The PBGC may file the petition regardless of whether there is a pending proceeding (1) involving bankruptcy, mortgage foreclosure or equity receivership, (2) to reorganize, conserve or liquidate the plan or its property, or (3) to enforce a lien against the plan's property.[30]

Furthermore, the court may stay any pending proceedings that involve plan property.[31] If the court agrees with the PBGC that the plan should be terminated, the court will then appoint a trustee, or authorize the existing trustee, to terminate the plan.

Alternatively, the PBGC and plan administrator may agree to terminate the plan without court proceedings.[32] There is no requirement under ERISA that plan participants and other interested parties receive notice or an opportunity to be heard prior to the PBGC and plan administrator coming to an agreement to terminate the plan.[33]

EMPLOYER LIABILITY

Standard Termination

In a standard termination, the plan sponsor has no further liability to the PBGC or plan participants. The plan sponsor may be able to recapture any assets remaining after participants have received their share, which is known as a "reversion."

A reversion may be subject to an excise tax at a 20% rate, which is increased to 50% if the plan sponsor does not take certain actions, such as establishing a qualified replacement plan.[34]

Distress Termination

In a distress termination, the plan sponsor and members of its controlled group are jointly and severally liable to the PBGC for the amount that the benefit liabilities exceed plan assets, with interest, at termination.[35] The PBGC will have a claim to recover at least some of these amounts. If successful, the PBGC will pay some of the recovery to plan participants as additional benefits and will keep the remaining amount to help cover its losses.

The employer's payment for the liability is due on the plan's termination date. The PBGC is authorized to make arrangements with the liable parties for the payments,[36] and any amount in excess of 30% of the collective net worth of the sponsor and controlled group will be paid under commercially reasonable terms.[37] In addition, the PBGC may claim a lien for up to 30% of the collective net worth of the sponsor and controlled group.[38] The PBGC may bring a civil action in U.S. district court to enforce the lien, which generally must be filed within six years of the plan's termination date. The lien has the same priority as a federal tax lien in section 6323 of the Internal Revenue Code and is treated as a federal tax lien in bankruptcy proceedings.[39]

Involuntary Termination

In an involuntary termination, the sponsor and controlled group are jointly and severally liable to the PBGC for the unfunded liabilities in the same manner as discussed above for a distress termination. The sponsor and controlled group are also liable to the trustee for the outstanding balance of the accumulated funding deficiencies, the outstanding balance of the funding deficiencies waived prior to termination, and the outstanding balance of the decreases in the minimum funding standard allowed prior to termination.[40] These amounts are due, plus interest, on the date of termination.

Attempt to Evade Liability

If a company sells or transfers a business with an underfunded pension plan in order to evade liability and the plan is ended within five years of the sale or transfer, ERISA provides that the company can still be treated as a contributing sponsor at the plan's termination date.[41] Thus, the company may be held liable for the unfunded liabilities.

ENFORCEMENT AND PENALTIES

The PBGC is broadly authorized to make any investigation it deems necessary to enforce ERISA[42] and may assess a penalty against anyone who fails to provide a required notice or other material information.[43] The penalty is limited to $1,000 for each day the failure occurs. In addition, plan participants, beneficiaries, fiduciaries, and sponsors who are adversely affected by an action of another (other than the PBGC) that violates the termination provisions may file suit in U.S. district court to enjoin the action or obtain other equitable relief.[44] Employee organizations representing affected participants and beneficiaries are also able to file a claim, and the PBGC has the right to intervene in any action.

PLAN RESTORATION

If the PBGC determines that a plan should not be terminated, it may stop the termination proceedings and restore the plan.[45] The PBGC may even restore a terminated plan. When determining whether a plan should be restored, the PBGC may look at subsequent pension plans sponsored by the employer.[46] The PBGC may be particularly interested in any subsequent plan that appears to be a "follow-on plan." A follow-on plan is designed so that when its benefits are added to the benefits being paid by the PBGC under the termination insurance program for the first plan, the total benefits are roughly the same as the first plan's benefits. Thus, the employees receive approximately what they expected to receive under the first plan, but the PBGC, rather than the employer, is responsible for paying some of the benefits.

End Notes

[1] Defined benefit plans are those where participants are promised a specified future benefit, which traditionally is an annuity beginning at retirement. For defined benefit plans, the employer bears the investment risk and is responsible for any shortfalls. ERISA § 3(35); 29 U.S.C. § 1002(35).

[2] A defined contribution plan is a pension plan in which the contributions are specified, but not the benefits. A defined contribution plan provides an individual account for each participant that accrues benefits based solely on the amount contributed to the account and any income,

expenses, and investment gains or losses to the account. See ERISA § 3(34); 29 U.S.C. § 1002(34).

[3] ERISA § 4021(b); 29 U.S.C. § 1321(b).

[4] ERISA § 4041(b); 29 U.S.C. § 1341(b).

[5] Affected parties include plan participants, beneficiaries (of deceased participants or alternate payees under a qualified domestic relations order), alternate payees under qualified domestic relations orders, employee organizations representing plan participants, and any person who has been designated to receive notice on behalf of an affected party. ERISA § 4001(a)(21); 29 U.S.C. § 1301(a)(21).

[6] ERISA § 4041(a)(2); 29 U.S.C. § 1341(a)(2); 29 C.F.R. § 4041.23(a).

[7] ERISA § 4041(b)(2)(A); 29 U.S.C. § 1341(b)(2)(A).

[8] ERISA § 4041(b)(2)(B); 29 U.S.C. § 1341(b)(2)(B).

[9] ERISA § 4041(b)(2)(C); 29 U.S.C. § 1341(b)(2)(C).

[10] ERISA § 4041(b)(3); 29 U.S.C. § 1341(b)(3).

[11] ERISA § 4050; 29 U.S.C. § 1350.

[12] ERISA § 4041(b)(3)(B); 29 U.S.C. § 1341(b)(3)(B).

[13] ERISA § 4041(c); 29 U.S.C. § 1341(c).

[14] For purposes of the plan termination provisions, "controlled group" means, in connection with any person, a group consisting of such person and all other persons under common control with such person," as determined under PBGC regulations. ERISA § 4001(a)(14); 29 U.S.C. § 1301(a)(14).

[15] The Pension Protection Act of 2006 (P.L. 109-280, § 404) amended the law to require that certain determinations, including the calculation of the plan participants' guarantied benefits, be made using the date the bankruptcy petition is filed, rather than the plan's actual termination date. ERISA §§ 4022(g), 4044(e); 29 U.S.C. §§ 1322(g), 1344(e). This affects both distress and involuntary terminations (discussed below), and one consequence is that post-bankruptcy accruals are no longer guarantied. In June 2011, the PBGC finalized regulations implementing the act's provisions. See Bankruptcy Filing Date Treated as Plan Termination Date for Certain Purposes, 76 Fed. Reg. 34590 (June 14, 2011) (codified at 29 C.F.R. Parts 4001, 4022, and 4044).

[16] ERISA § 4041(c)(2)(B); 29 U.S.C. § 1341(c)(2)(B).

[17] ERISA § 4041(a)(2); 29 U.S.C. § 1341(a)(2); 29 C.F.R. § 4041.43(a).

[18] ERISA § 4041(c)(2)(A); 29 U.S.C. § 1341(c)(2)(A). This additional information must be provided to other affected parties no later than 15 days after (1) the receipt of a request for the information or (2) the provision of new information to the PBGC relating to a previous request. ERISA § 4041(c)(2)(D); 29 U.S.C. § 1341(c)(2)(D).

[19] ERISA § 4041(c)(2)(C); 29 U.S.C. § 1341(c)(2)(C).

[20] ERISA § 4041(c)(3)(B)(i); 29 U.S.C. § 1341(c)(3)(B)(i).

[21] ERISA § 4041(c)(3)(B)(ii); 29 U.S.C. § 1341(c)(3)(B)(ii).

[22] ERISA § 4041(c)(3)(B)(iii); 29 U.S.C. § 1341(c)(3)(B)(iii).

[23] ERISA § 4041(c)(3)(C); 29 U.S.C. § 1341(c)(3)(C).

[24] ERISA § 4050; 29 U.S.C. § 1350.

[25] ERISA § 4042; 29 U.S.C. § 1342.

[26] ERISA § 4042(a); 29 U.S.C. §1342(a).

[27] ERISA § 4042(b); 29 U.S.C. §1342(b).

[28] ERISA § 4042(d); 29 U.S.C. § 1342(d).

[29] ERISA § 4042(c)(1); 29 U.S.C. § 1342(c)(1).

[30] ERISA § 4042(e); 29 U.S.C. § 1342(e).

[31] ERISA § 4042(f); 29 U.S.C. § 1342(f).
[32] ERISA § 4042(c)(1); 29 U.S.C. § 1342(c)(1).
[33] See In Re Jones & Laughlin Hourly Pension Plan v. LTV Steel Co., 824 F.2d 197 (2nd Cir. 1987).
[34] Internal Revenue Code § 4980.
[35] ERISA § 4062(b)(1); 29 U.S.C. § 1362(b)(1).
[36] ERISA § 4067; 29 U.S.C. § 1367.
[37] ERISA § 4062(b)(2)(B); 29 U.S.C. § 1362(b)(2)(B).
[38] ERISA § 4068; 29 U.S.C. § 1368.
[39] ERISA § 4068(c); 29 U.S.C. § 1368(c).
[40] ERISA § 4062(c); 29 U.S.C. § 1362(c).
[41] ERISA § 4069; 29 U.S.C. § 1369.
[42] ERISA § 4003(a); 29 U.S.C. § 1303(a).
[43] ERISA §4071; 29 U.S.C. § 1371.
[44] ERISA § 4070; 29 U.S.C. § 1370.
[45] ERISA § 4047; 29 U.S.C. § 1347.
[46] See PBGC v. LTV Corp., 496 U.S. 633 (1990).

INDEX

F

G

H

I

J

L

M

N

O

P